The Heart Too Long Suppressed *A Chronicle of Mental Illness*

The Heart Too Long Suppressed *A Chronicle of Mental Illness*

Carol Hebald

Northeastern University Press
Boston

Northeastern University Press

Copyright 2001 by Carol Hebald

Some of the names in this book have been changed.

Library of Congress Cataloging-in-Publication Data
Hebald, Carol.
The heart too long suppressed : a chronicle of mental illness / Carol Hebald.
p. cm.
ISBN 1-55553-482-1 (cloth : alk. paper)
1. Hebald, Carol. 2. English teachers—United States—Biography. 3. Psychiatric
hospital patients—United States—Biography. 4. Mentally ill women—United
States—Biography. 5. Authors, American—20th century—Biography. I. Title.
PE64.H38 A3 2001
616.89′0092—dc21
[B]   2001018337

Designed by Joyce C. Weston

Composed in Minion by The Composing Room of Michigan, Inc.,
Grand Rapids, Michigan. Printed and bound by The Maple Press,
York, Pennsylvania. The paper is Sebago Antique, an acid-free stock.

MANUFACTURED IN THE UNITED STATES OF AMERICA
05 04 03 02 01   5 4 3 2 1

This book is dedicated to the psychiatrist who told me, "There's no doubt in my mind you'll take your own life. It's only a question of time."

For spite, I'm not doing it.

First Prayer

The heart, too long suppressed,
cannot come forth,
finds comfort in memories of snow,
in poems that grieve to grow.

Then stir my slow conception,
quiet, oh how quiet,
the tides resume in me,
thrust me back to see

the soul outside my mind,
thrice-blessed,
released from what it longs for
to something it has.

I live in a dreamworld by choice;
I am sorry,
slightly embarrassed
and ravished.

Contents

Foreword DR. THOMAS SZASZ

*T*his is the memoir of a woman who might conventionally be called a "former mental patient." There are countless books by ex-patients. What is special about Carol Hebald's? That she is a talented writer, instinctively aware that she writes because she wants her Voice to be heard and recognized as legitimate, because she wants to "outshout" the voices that have demeaned and oppressed her—to which, at one time, she mistakenly listened. That may be why she wrote this book. But why should anyone read it? Because it is a good read is by no means the only reason. More important, Hebald's moving account dramatically illustrates the dangers of letting the voice of authority outshout your Inner Voice: she effectively demonstrates that the sole recovery possible from the maladies a person so acquires is to regain the voice he or she has not so much lost as renounced. Near the end of her story, Hebald confronts her psychiatrist with *her* perception of *him*. His response: "Lower your voice!"

Ironically, we pride ourselves on being rational, especially about matters of health. But we have become quite irrational about understanding people, a subject we think of as a matter of mental health. Many people—especially writers and poets—have struggled to expose this error characteristic of our age. The great Russian linguist Mikhail Bakhtin was an important fighter in this, presently losing, struggle. "The human sciences," he observed, "are the sciences of man in his specificity, and not the sciences of a *voiceless* thing. . . ." Moreover, Bakhtin was keenly aware of how dependent every one of us is on the voice of the Other: "No member of a verbal community can ever find words in the language that are neutral, exempt from the aspirations and evaluations of the other, uninhabited by the other's voice." We are fated to attend to, assimilate, and make use of the voices of others—and yet maintain a voice of our own. It is no small task.

We are wont to refer to the dominant obsession of a particular period in shorthand, as the Age of Faith, the Age of Reason, or the Age of Anxiety. In that style, the period since the end of World War II may be dubbed the Age of Understanding or, perhaps better, the Age of Misunderstanding, exemplified by former President William Jefferson Clinton's memorable phrase, "I feel your pain." That, as everyone realizes, is the last thing a president feels or can be expected to feel. But it is the lie many of us want to hear.

No one—especially no parent or psychiatrist—acknowledges that he does not understand his children or patients, much less that he *does not want to understand them.* Yet, that is the truth that hurried parents hide behind the rhetoric of "quality time," and psychiatrists behind the rhetoric of "treating mental illness."

What do we mean when we say that we want to understand another person? We can only mean that we want to grasp how and what he thinks and feels, about himself and the world. There is only one way to do that, namely, by *listening to his Voice.* That is easier said than done. Why? Because it takes Time, a commodity we moderns either pride ourselves about not having enough of (in which case we feel important because we are "busy") or complain about having too much of and not knowing what to do with (in which case we feel bored, and others are likely to call us "depressed," perhaps even "suicidal"). Furthermore, listening to the Other is hard work, because every voice articulates its own

perception of reality, likely to conflict with the perception artic-
ulated by the listener's inner voice. The upshot is that few people
really listen. That is why listening to the Other is one of the surest
ways of gaining the speaker's affection and trust, and why, if
we want to gain "insight" into how people think, feel, and live,
reading literature beats psychology and psychiatry hands down.
W. H. Auden put it much better when he wrote, "Writers can be
guilty of every kind of human conceit but one, the conceit of the
social worker: 'We are all here on earth to help others; what on
earth the others are here for, I don't know.'"

Many are here to recover from such "help." Carol Hebald gives
Voice to them and shows them the Way.

Thomas Szasz
Professor of Psychiatry Emeritus
State University of New York, Upstate Medical University
Syracuse, New York

ACKNOWLEDGMENTS

Excerpts from *The Heart Too Long Suppressed,* including my poem "First Prayer," were published in *Confrontation* #56/57.

For technical support I am most deeply indebted to John Turner. I also extend warm thanks to Shirley Onacilla and George Cominskie.

For their patience and moral support during the difficult process of writing, I am most grateful to Dr. Thomas Szasz and Professor Loree Rackstraw.

For editorial suggestions on an early draft, I thank Herbert Reich.

For facts about my paternal heritage, thanks to my cousins Milton Hebald, Mildred Birnbaum, and Margo Hebald.

For their editorial expertise, I am deeply grateful to my editor, Elizabeth Swayze, and my agent, Thomas Wallace.

Finally, I am indebted to the Virginia Center for the Creative Arts for the long weeks of silence that enabled me to think through a final draft.

Prologue

*I*n the summer of 1978, while accompanying my mother and her third husband on a ten-week pleasure cruise to Leningrad, I threw overboard the following medications: the psychotropic tranquilizers Haldol and Thorazine and the antidepressants Imipramine Daytime and Tofranil P.M. A psychiatric patient in and out of hospitals for thirty years, I'd been on massive doses of medication for twenty. I was forty-four.

The previous fall I'd begun my job as assistant professor of English and creative writing at the University of Kansas, at Lawrence. It had become my habit, as a visiting university lecturer, to register upon arriving in town at the nearest medical facility with a note from my former therapist indicating the pills I was taking. It was up to me to find a doctor who'd consent to rewrite my prescriptions and take me on as a patient. Given my medical history, not everyone would.

The nearest facility to Lawrence is the renowned Menninger Clinic, in Topeka, where I was promptly scheduled for a morning-long battery of psychological tests. One of the reasons I'd accepted the job in Kansas was that at Menninger's I hoped to find a lasting cure for whatever it was that ailed me.

The administering psychologist, Dr. Sheila Skollar, summoned me from the waiting area at 8:30 A.M. and began with a brief apology for having to ask me, as a mere formality, some rather stupid routine questions. I smiled.

"Who is the president of the United States?" she asked.

I opened my mouth to speak.—Carter's name escaped my mind. I froze, then laughed or tried to, as I explained that I had just arrived in this blistering August heat from the MacDowell Artists' Colony in New Hampshire, where I'd been working round the clock on a novel that was beginning finally, *finally* to take shape. I laughed again. Just one second more and I'd remember . . . Dr. Skollar suggested we get on with the Rorschach and word-association tests. I answered carefully and thoroughly—too thoroughly perhaps to compensate for my memory lapse because twice she admonished sharply, "Just say what you see!"

By lunchtime we had finished. "I'll be straight with you," she said. "You seem extremely disorganized."

"I'm tired!"

"I think it's more than that. Look, I don't think you can give a coherent lecture. I'm recommending your hospitalization."

"What? For *what?*" I was shocked. "Dr. Skollar, I'm starting a new job next week! Teaching's how I support myself. Please! I've just been overworking. I can rest at home."

"I don't think so," she said.

Then, "How am I supposed to pay a hospital bill without the medical insurance the job provides?"

She assured me that something could be worked out.

"You really think I need . . . ?" A lump in my throat stopped me. "I don't know what to do first," I said, finally, "go home and pack, or telephone my chairman immediately." The tears welled up.

Appeased, she seemed at once kinder. "Look, you have my opinion," she said sensibly. "I'll pass it on to Dr. Sampson" (the psychiatrist to whom I'd been assigned). "You're seeing him tomorrow?" I nodded. "Then just do nothing until tomorrow. If he agrees with me, we'll take it from there."

It was lunchtime. Since I didn't drive, I had to take the Lawrence bus, which didn't leave for a couple of hours. I asked her where I could get a bite to eat.

"They're eating downstairs right now," she said. "I'll arrange for you to join them as a visitor."

I stood in line with the inpatients, pleasant looking, mostly young—none recognizably ill. But few mental patients at the elite retreats are. It struck me that no one bothered to ask if I was new. There were no locked doors. I was visiting today, that's all. But in a day or two I'd be "in again." I felt discouraged and so horribly tired that, were it not for my teaching contract and the probability of a ruined career, which Dr. Skollar dismissed so very lightly ("Your health comes first!"), I'd have taken her advice without question.

Horribly tired, did I say? Then why suddenly on that lunch queue did my heart begin to pound, my muscles to freeze? My arms grew stiff—one began lifting of its own accord—when I turned around, mounted the stairs, and ran far, far down the road as fast as I could until I reached the bus stop. I sat down to rest.

Across the street was an empty phone booth. I had with me the number of a fellow artist in whom I'd confided at MacDowell. A prominent critic and novelist, she had attended an after-dinner reading I'd given from my novella *Asylum*, about a mental patient's struggle for self-possession. When my friend asked its source, I answered, personal experience. She then read the complete novella and claimed to be deeply moved by it. I was honored. We swam together, ate together, and talked intimately.

I told her, because she asked, that aside from a brief year of marriage, I'd lived my adult life alone, and that I was on heavy medication because I was troubled by visions of Jesus. In fact, the previous year, when I taught at the University of Wisconsin, my visions were followed by a searing pain in one eye and temporary blindness.

But why did I admit this to a stranger? Because I was in desperate need of a friend. And because in such states of desperation, we trust whomever we need. Half expecting to be betrayed, we are sometimes wonderfully surprised. Before the onset of my blindness, I had shared my terror of these visions with my former dean at Utica College, a trained psychologist, who advised me wisely not to be afraid, that they might portend something positive. It occurred to me then that it was my fear of insanity, and not the visions themselves, that had caused my blindness and pain.

But I must have frightened my friend from MacDowell, whose interest in me soon after cooled. I was really a bit heartbroken, but I was used to it. Another deposit for the memory bank, I thought. Or as Emerson more aptly put it, "Pearls and rubies to [his] discourse."* Once, I fell in love with someone whose best friend told me, confidentially, of course, "He doesn't want anyone that sick."

My MacDowell friend picked up the phone with a gracious hello. I got quickly to the point about my recommended hospitalization. "So I'll probably be writing to you from Topeka, not Lawrence," I said. "I'm really sorry to lay this on you."

"You're not laying anything on me," she replied, "because there's nothing I can do."

It was then I decided to fight.

I knew that the next day my psychiatrist, Dr. Sampson, hearing the customary factual rundown of my life, would be on the lookout for "disorganized thinking." So with nothing to do that night, I prepared my life history. Never deviating from facts, I would pause at strategic places and toss in a few insights into the

---

*From his essay "The American Scholar," in which he adds, "Drudgery, calamity, exasperation, want, are instructors in eloquence and wisdom."

probable causes of my illness. I began with the death of my father when I was four, followed by my inability to listen in school,
or to read until I was nine.

"Where *were* you?" asked the doctor next day.

"I can't say for sure . . . probably in an unconscious fantasy of
heaven. Or at least knocking at the gate. I *do* remember thinking
'Our Father, who art in heaven' was my father in particular."

"And you were his special child?"

"Well, I liked to think so," I answered modestly.

Dr. Sampson smiled. I had passed, I assumed splendidly, since
he disagreed with Dr. Skollar's recommendation, and backed my
decision to go home and prepare my classes.

I traveled to Topeka weekly to see him, took my medications
faithfully, and began teaching at the University of Kansas. At the
end of the academic year, I received a note from my chairman:
my student evaluations for fall and spring semesters had been
outstanding. If I wanted to be considered for early promotion
and tenure, he'd be happy to support me.

Dr. Sampson was delighted by my chairman's encouragement.
"We're doing very well," he beamed.

All year, my feelings of loneliness had been acute. I'd call
him—not often, but from time to time. "Get a dog," he told me.
"There's nothing wrong with loving a dog!"

"Can I call you again?" I asked him.

"What do you want me to tell you?" he joked. "Get a cat?"

But what did I expect? I had wanted above all to write. If romantic relationships weren't possible for me, close friendships
were. And if there was no one yet within shouting distance, I'd
nourish myself on books and music. I worked beyond en-
durance. Nothing was happening! I was harping on the same old
subjects. Thoughts spun on the wheels of thought. I clutched at

possibilities. And the train ground down to a halt. My mind was in a groove.

Shortly before summer recess, when I agreed to join my parents on their cruise, I asked Dr. Sampson if he thought I'd ever be well enough to function without therapy and medication. He answered that I'd *probably* have to continue the former indefinitely; I'd need the pills for the rest of my life.

I had been ready to give up, to settle. I even took a perverse pride, each time the dosage was increased, in how well I still could function. Despite Thorazine's annoying side effects, for me, a parched mouth and sandpaper tongue (students ribbed me about the two diet sodas always on my desk), I was seldom absent from class. My hospitalizations occurred between semesters and during holidays. I was remarkably well controlled, really something of a wunderkind.

But that year things had changed. "Medications for the rest of my life?" I echoed.

"You're doing very well," he insisted.

"For a sick person?" He didn't respond. "Tell me, do those pills inhibit the imagination?"

"They inhibit delusional thinking," he replied.

"Which is seated in the imagination, no? Doctor, that's my stock-in-trade," I yelled.

"Just be grateful we have them." Then, "Are you forgetting the night terrors, the hallucinations?"

"You're absolutely certain they *are* hallucinations?"

"There's no doubt in my mind."

We ended the session.

The following day, I called his secretary to cancel all future appointments. Two weeks later, on the high seas, I tossed my medications overboard. I've not taken a pill or seen a therapist since.

My terror and blindness are gone. And my visions, which abated in 1998, shortly before my mother's death, I have since learned were "benign." My former dean had hinted as much when she told me not to be frightened. But Dr. Sampson's reminder of my terror served only to reinforce it. *Hallucination* is a frightening word. Psychopaths "ordered by God to kill" claim to suffer from them. Did Dr. Sampson have a stake in keeping me dependent? If I thought so, why didn't I ask him? Because I was certain he'd assume the question symptomatic of my disease.

I was first hospitalized in the late fifties with paranoid schizophrenia, a psychosis characterized by intellectual deterioration, delusions, hallucinations, inattentiveness, and emotional dysfunction. Given that schizophrenia in its various subtypes was the psychiatric diagnosis of choice, with which a great many Americans were then hospitalized, I wondered why the possibility of my *mis*diagnosis was never raised. In 1978 I still wore the label. Whether I'd ever embodied it, I don't know. I knew only that I had to shed it. But *how?*

You and I and most other people have only one foothold in the world and that is the truth. But to live exclusively in reality is as intolerable as it is incomprehensible. For me it was seldom possible. Why? Was the truth so appalling? It's one thing to know it and another to tell it. Often I'd lie close to it. For example, my father died when I was four, but for many years I told people I was three. I thought if I exaggerated my early troubles, my amazed listener would think, "Look how well she's done despite them!" But to make a liar of myself for the sake of one year? Wasn't there another reason? To admit the facts surrounding my father's death would force me to relive them. And this I could not do. But with the crusting over of painful memories my illness took root. Who was I? I was the name I was given. I had an age, a sex, a profession. But there was no self to fall back on. Others couldn't relate to me.

Should I be ashamed to concede that people with worse beginnings than mine have fared better, when the converse is also true? We have different psychic strengths. I went crazy; you may not have. What's crazy? Not seeing, not caring to see . . . what? The effects of our early abuses, or the abusers themselves? Those who punished us not for our misdeeds but from their own misery, or those who remained apathetic? But apathy is madness too: When we endure too many insults in silence, we become indifferent to everything. And so gradually do we come to this condition we don't realize the full horror of it.

"Carol, for God's sake!" chided colleagues, sensing my despair. "They're starving in India!" And I wondered whether starving together made it any easier.

Clearly I needed help. But from whom? A healthy, competent professional, strong and skillful enough to awaken in me a clear memory of all I had buried. In thirty years of therapy I'd had one. My difficulties shared were lessened by half. By then I was middle-aged. What remained was the painful realization that in my adult life I had been responsible for the cruelest self-neglect because I couldn't help appeasing those in my early childhood who'd treated me precisely the same way.

PART ONE ~

Chapter One

The "memory" of my birth in 1934 grew out of the story my mother repeated so often, I felt myself a conscious witness to it:

"Hold back! Hold back!" cried Dr. Friedson. "She'll tear you to pieces!" I was traveling to life that quickly. When I arrived, and was properly whacked, the doctor lifted me up before her and announced, "A well-knit body!"

"I don't care, I don't care," moaned Mother, "as long as she's out of me."

When my father, who'd hoped fervently for a son, heard the news, "I have a daughter," he snapped.

"You have another one," said the nurse.

"Go to hell!"

But, according to Mother, he adored me. "Don't you remember him kissing your little hands and feet?"

"What? At six months old?"

"Six weeks!"

Now, how in heaven's name could I remember that?

~

Little has been passed on to me about my father: Bald, chubby Henry Hebald, the youngest of five sons, came from a long line of Polish watchmakers. Born in Kraków in 1882, he was, despite his lack of schooling, fluent in French, German, Hebrew, and English. His parents and baby sister remained in Poland as one by one his older brothers, reaching the age of conscription, emigrated to the States. Henry was the last to arrive. Four opened

3

separate jewelry stores: one in Brooklyn, the other three within sight of one another on Manhattan's Bowery. The fifth brother, Bernard, unable to make a go of things, turned up at the others' houses and pleaded with them for a job. They offered him dinner instead. "I just ate," said proud Bernard. But couldn't he sweep their stores after hours? No, they couldn't afford it; times were bad. A short time later Bernard killed himself.

The remaining brothers competed fiercely. Each would send his clerk out on trumped-up errands to the others' stores: "Go see how many customers Nathan has." "Go find out what time Julius is closing." The Bowery jewelers worked twelve-hour shifts, from ten in the morning until ten at night, seven days a week. Before he married, my father lived in the back of his store, where he'd take his women to bed. Unfriendly competitors called him "whore-master."

⌇

My mother, Ethel Miller, was born in 1901 on New York's Lower East Side. Her parents, Morris and Dora, were from Vilna—"*White Russia*," she was certain to point out. With Morris, a garment worker routinely on strike, Dora became a bootlegger. "She chose me as her little lookout," Ethel would boast in her later years. "I was only nine years old." And then she'd tell me the story:

"'Anyone out there?' called Mama, capping the last of the bottles. We couldn't be a second late. When the cop on the beat wasn't looking, we sent them down the dumbwaiter, and up came the empties. We hauled them in the window fast: 'Find the bottle with the yellow tissue paper,' yelled Mama. In it was our money for food. And if the bums cheated us out of it, what could we do? Nothing!" she bristled. Whatever Mother remembered she seemed to live anew:

"When summer came, I used to watch out our tenement window for the girls in white dresses marching to graduation. One day I begged, 'Mama, dress me in white. I want to graduate, too.' But she was bottling the bathtub gin. 'Don't pester me, pester Papa,' she hollered. But my father was praying; I couldn't interrupt him either. I cried so hard Mama raised her hand to smack me, but I was breaking her heart, she just couldn't. Guess what she did."

"Tell me!"

Her bent body perched slightly forward, Mother's gimlet eye glittered at the memory. "She grabbed the white sheet off the bed, folded and pinned it around me like a toga. Oh I looked like a little queen! 'Go!' ordered Mama. 'Go show off on the stoop.' And there I sat till evening, waving down the strangers. 'Hey! I graduated today.'" Mother sighed deeply.

"Go on."

"What for? You know the rest. . . . How I quit school at thirteen and took a job sweeping factory floors. Someone had to put food on the table. Me! I skipped three times! I was A-plus in composition! The insults I swallowed. They called me stupid. For what? Every Friday another pink slip." She'd shake her head at the memory, the tears rolling down her cheeks.

Times were so hard, she told me, that her cousin gave piano lessons by day on the same instrument he slept on at night—without ever having learned a note! He advertised for advanced students only, whose auditions he'd conduct as follows: "Legato . . . portato . . . staccato . . . shhhhhh—pianissimo! Largo . . . larghetto . . . and fa-la, fa-la-la—not bad, not bad! Once again?"

When Morris was on strike, he and his Orthodox friends would sit around the kitchen table drinking tea and discussing Torah. Never once did Mother speak of him to me. I asked her why.

"He was close to my older sister Fanny. Whenever we misbehaved, he hit her, not me." She sounded jealous.

"But whose fault was it, usually?"

"Mine," she admitted sheepishly. "My father was afraid of me."

Afraid of what? That the sole supporter of his family could also speak her mind? When he caught Mother cooking bacon on the Sabbath, he warned her that God would punish her. "Really?" she tossed back. "How?"

"He'll take ten years from your life."

"That's all?"

In a snapshot of my mother taken in the summer of '22, she's seated on a park bench, smiling. Impeccably dressed in a full plaid skirt and belted jacket—Dora made all her children's clothes—she resembles a tender young queen.

She was twenty. Having graduated from factory girl to stenographer, she worked down the hall from Louis Goldman, a handsome young dentist with whom she made a lunchtime appointment. Sweeping in the door, she told him, "Make it fast. If you see a cavity, fill it. Don't scrape me any new ones with your instrument." He looked at her a moment, then laughed. And so began their seven-year courtship.

"Her *Goldmankey*," jeered Dora, who took refuge from her loveless marriage every Saturday afternoon at the Yiddish Theater, then reenacted the entire play verbatim at home. A superb mimic, she'd switch parts, bounce from chair to chair, and send the family to bed "laughing through their tears." Mother worshipped her. Years later, when Dora asked her to fund Fanny's piano lessons from her secretarial paycheck, and eventually also to cede her dowry, Mother said she didn't mind. "I was pretty, Fanny wasn't. And she was older by a year and a half. She had to catch a husband somehow."

Fanny was gifted at the piano. She was only ten when our relative, the poet and minstrel Eliakum Zunser, asked her to play his songs at a neighborhood wedding. As a young lady, Fanny was too nervous to work; that's what they called it in those days. She tried her hand at a few clerical jobs. But the clatter of multiple typewriters in the narrow, airless offices of the day scrambled her thoughts so badly she couldn't organize her files.

"Several women in our family were born deaf, dumb, and blind," Mother repeatedly told me. "We feared for Fanny's mind. One summer morning Fanny complained, 'It seems to me there's a big hole in the middle of the kitchen floor.' The doctor ordered her to quit her job and swim at the free beach in Coney Island. So the poor thing went by herself every day on the subway. At night we shared the same bed, went together once a week to the public baths." Mother stopped in the midst of her thought. "Don't you ever tell that to anyone."

"You're ashamed of *that?*" I asked, amazed. "But you were a heroine, you struggled!"

"Just keep your mouth shut, that's all."

Continuing to support the whole family, Mother would come home exhausted, only to find her two younger brothers in bed, staring at the ceiling. When Dora told her the boys were depressed, "If my brothers are depressed," snapped Mother, "it's because they resent me for working."

She was twenty-six when her beloved Louis jilted her for a young lady of means. Fanny had no boyfriend, either. So on Saturday nights, the sisters would stay home and hang out separate windows to cry. One night Fanny blew her nose loudly, and, finding Ethel's eye on her, turned quickly away, then back—both caught in paroxysms of laugher.

Mother did secretarial work for the renowned bowel specialist Dr. Brinkler. Besieged with pleas for nutritional advice from all over the country, he allowed her to answer his mail. She loved her job, and had earned enough for the Millers to move up to the elegant Bronx.

One Saturday, she and Fanny went downtown to choose a wedding gift for a mutual friend. As soon as they stepped into Henry's store, they found it. As Fanny made out the check, bald, smiling Henry sidled up to Ethel. "Aren't you a bookkeeper?" he asked, by which he meant, Can't you write?

"No," she replied proudly. "I analyze sick people's complaints."

"Like a doctor?"

"Like a doctor."

And Henry fell in love. That night, at nine o'clock, he called her: "I had a date I didn't like. I took her home."

"So? Where are you?"

"Downstairs in a booth. Could I come up?"

"I'm not dressed! Neither is my mother."

"*Get* dressed."

Dora was ironing in the kitchen, and Ethel waiting in the parlor, when fifteen minutes later the bell rang. Dora peeped out for a quick hello and withdrew to let the lovers get acquainted. Henry began with a kiss.

"What *is* this?" asked Mother, edging away on the couch. Henry stared at his spats. A moment later he tried again, when she rose and announced regally, "If it was in my mind to see you again, Mr. Hebald, I've changed it."

Highly insulted, Henry opened the closet door.

"No, the other one," Mother pointed. And he left.

"So fast?" asked Dora, racing in from the kitchen.

"He touched me," complained Ethel.

"He touched you!" mocked Grandma. "What are you afraid

of? He'll take a chunk out of your hip and not return it? You're twenty-six years old!"

"Want to see me get him back?"

Henry had had the sniffles. So Mother spent Sunday writing him an essay entitled "How to Cure a Cold," signed Professor Miller. They married in 1928. He was forty-six; she, twenty-seven. The night before the wedding, she sobbed inconsolably to her mother. Still in love with Louis, she never liked Henry to touch her. "Go to a whore," she would tell him.

⁓

Soon after my birth, Mother gained fifty pounds. Her neighbors on East Fourth Street would peek in on her at midday, and finding her still in her nightgown and the house a shambles, would chide, "Ethel! You only had a baby!"

"Only?"

"Aren't you breast-feeding? Why not?"

Mother explained that she'd had such a hard time nursing my older sister, she had no milk for me. A colicky baby, Janice had bitten her. *I'd* be raised by the book: I'd have my bottle on time and not a minute sooner, nor would she pay attention when I cried. It was never too early to teach the difficult art of forbearance.

How was it, having worked for Dr. Brinkler, Mother didn't know that infants can't control their sphincter muscles? Beaten into toilet training, Jani learned much faster than I. My daily "accomplishments" were thereafter compared with hers.

Jan always insisted I was an unusually beautiful child. Four years my senior, she felt by comparison unusually ugly. "Did you know," she reminded me recently, "that Mother never let us crawl?"

"Why not? Was the floor dirty?"

9

"No, she was crazy clean! Except after you were born, when she let the house go to pot. Ate everything in sight, even your baby food."

She let me cry from hunger, then ate my food? What was wrong? She missed working. Henry forbade it. Instead, he hired our maid Mary, who, when concerned neighbors persuaded Mother to join them for an outing, would lock me in a dark closet before I was one year old. When Jan, sensing something wrong, told Mother, the two kicked Mary bodily out the door. Later they agreed I was not only an unusually beautiful child, but an unusually quiet one, too.

~

In the beginning, my father felt only a little tired and had lost his too-hearty appetite. When his complexion began to yellow, Dr. Friedson took one look at him and knew: he had liver cancer. In keeping with the custom of the day, the diagnosis was withheld from him. He rested at home. It was 1937; I was three. Seven-year-old Jan was in second grade when Mother took charge of his jewelry store.

He'd call me often to his room. I'd creep into his bed, where he read to me from his new edition of *The Complete Works of William Shakespeare*. How he loved to shake his forefinger at me and in singing words declaim, "Better a witty fool than a foolish wit," or "How sharper than a serpent's tooth it is / To have a thankless child." He was in bed for a year. We spent our days together. When his nurse knocked on the door, he'd yell, "Stay out, I'm with my daughter."

I recalled in a flashback twenty years later in a psychiatrist's office that my father had made love to me.

One afternoon my cousin, the sculptor Milton Hebald, then a boy of nineteen, visited Father with his first finished work in hand. The two had been extremely close. Milton was six when his own father, Nathan (my father's brother), was gunned down by thieves at his store. My father, then a bachelor, moved in with Nathan's family and, according to Jewish tradition, was expected to marry his widow. Daddy wouldn't. But he loved to watch little Milton carve figurines out of Ivory soap and drop the shavings on the floor for his mother and older sisters to pick up. Everyone but my father had disapproved his "hobby."

"Well, Uncle?" Milton asked him on his deathbed.

Daddy examined the sculpture carefully. "It's very good, Milton," he said finally, "but carve the 'Hebald' a little bigger."

One day Father overheard the doctor tell my mother, "He doesn't have much time." Soon he was in too much pain to see me. Toward the end, I heard his great shout in the night, "God, don't let me die."

I saw him one last time. "Daddy, what should I be when I grow up?"

"Be somebody."

"Who?"

I remember our days together as the most idyllic of my life. We did more than make love; we read Shakespeare. I have never, to this day, been able to muster the appropriate rage I'm supposed to have felt. I find it impossible to hate the man whose agonized screams still echo in my ears. He died in September 1938.

Just as his illness was kept from him, his death was kept from me. The day of the funeral, Janice and I were sent to the movies. Later, when I asked, "Where's Daddy?" Mother told me, "Daddy went far away on a long, long trip."

Soon after I got sick myself, and Dr. Friedson was summoned to the house: "Open wide—ahhhh!"

"Ahhhh."

"Well?" asked Mother.

"She has to have her tonsils out," he announced.

I grabbed onto his pants leg: "Do you want to be my daddy?" I asked. Silent, he looked from Mother to me. I wouldn't let go. I suppose she called me off—I don't remember the details—but I knew I'd moved them both, and for the first time, savored a feeling of power.

The day Mother checked me out of the hospital, she dropped me at home in a taxi and rode straight to the store. No sooner had I opened the door than Jan hugged me tight. She'd missed me! I'd missed her, too. She didn't know she was holding me so tight. I cried from pain, "Stop!" And she began smacking me on the head with both hands.

Daddy had been gone only a few months when I saw her standing on a windy street, crying. It was winter, and she was alone. She thought Mother didn't love her. Sometimes she'd stutter, and Mother would smack her to stop. Then, in her presence, she'd call me her "little ray of sunshine."

Suddenly, Jani was hitting me hard:

"Why did you use my towel?"

"I didn't."

"You did."

"I didn't."

"You did." (Yes, I did.)

She was slapping me on the head with both hands. The quick sharp stings, the stunning shocks—I couldn't catch my breath. She took my head and banged it against the wall, then kicked me hard in the stomach. I couldn't stop crying, couldn't tell her I'd made a mistake.

One night in our common bedroom I woke to find her snipping off my eyelashes. After she fell asleep, I tried to stick a knitting needle into her eyes—when catching it, she aimed it at mine. I was rushed to the doctor's office. "Carol tried to hurt herself," explained Jan. Of course she was believed. She believes it to this day.

~

Mother walked from the house to the store, where she worked my father's grueling hours. A Junoesque, Roman-nosed beauty of thirty-seven, her auburn hair swept up in stylish pompadour, she dressed for business every morning in the same mannish suit: khaki one week, brown the next. I'd follow her from room to room, watch her roll on her stockings, struggle into her corset, then fasten it hook by hook. "What's that?" I'd ask. "That child is always following me around," she complained. "That child is always asking questions." But they were vitally important to me!

Soon after, I'd open my mouth to speak, only to lose my thought. On the verge of it again, I couldn't catch it. Again I'd try, and again, opening and shutting my mouth, until Mother screamed, "What is it you want?" Then, "This is you." She mimicked a fish drowning in air. When I lost objects too, she'd cluck, "Just like my sister Fanny." But it was Fanny, in the far-off Bronx, who took me into her arms the week my father died; Fanny, in her egg-stained housedress, who allowed me the blessed relief of tears. Flesh, not words, I wanted.

One morning, I'd found something to do! I was cutting up paper with a pair of scissors. Pleased and proud, I cried. "Look Mommy—look what I'm doing!"

"Only crazy people do that," she said.

Silent and forgetful, I began to suck my lip. "You'll get cancer like Daddy," she warned. But I couldn't stop. "Over and over, Carol, like a monkey?" She'd mimic with a crooked face.

With no toys ("What do they need toys for?"), I played with pots and pans while our Hungarian maid, Barbara, ate breakfast.

"Where's Mommy?" No answer.

I wandered from room to room. I looked out all the windows, opened all the doors. I couldn't stop moving, I couldn't stop searching.

Sometimes I'd cut myself for an excuse to bother her at the store. I couldn't tell her the other reasons. Constipated, I was given strong laxatives and often lost control. This made Barbara so furious, she housebroke me like a dog by putting my nose in it and smacking me.

Every morning after Mother left, Barbara would sweep the floor quickly, nervously. She wanted to be done! I grabbed onto the end of her broom. "Pay attention to me!" She hit me with it. I screamed. She hit me again. I screamed louder. Then she pushed me into a dark closet, just as Mary had, and locked it with a key.

Did I bang to get out? I don't remember. My entrance into fantasy was swift. The first is vivid in my mind: A fat lady, living by myself in the woods, I never changed out of my nightgown. Every morning a delivery boy would arrive with a huge bag of groceries at my door. From behind it, I'd hand him his payment and tip. Then I'd eat alone all day long.

I tried to think down the hours. The morning was sharp and clear. Now it was dark and close. I held myself, rocking back and forth, back and forth. I wished, and then believed, someone was rocking me. A sleeve became my father's hand; a silk dress, my mother's breast; a fur coat, my father's chest. But here I must confess, even as I write this, my mind is traveling elsewhere, as it must have then when sorrow split off en route and left only memory charged with longing.

Barbara must have let me out before Jan came home from school. It happened daily; I told no one. Barbara said she'd kill me if I did.

Not yet five, I chose my night dreams too: A bald, chubby man resembling Daddy welcomed me at the circus gate.

"What'll it be tonight?" he'd ask: "A circus or a spanking?"

"Too many bums in the circus," I'd say. I chose the spanking instead. It gave me immense pleasure. Pudgyman did the honors.

So from night's darkness I entered the day's.

∼

A Hungarian-Jewish refugee, lonely, pockmarked Barbara joined "over twenty-eight" clubs to meet men. Weeknights she'd seek my mother's advice: to kiss or not to kiss? Or . . . and then they'd whisper things. I took pleasure listening in. One Saturday morning Barbara took me into her maid's room bed. Peering down her pajama top, I saw a dark, pink nipple large as the cover of our soup tureen. I reached to touch it; she hugged me fiercely. Is it possible this brutal woman loved me? Yes, as one loves a little kitten one beats in rage for yowling. In rage? Why? My needs were too sharp a reminder of her own. I knew that even then.

Now, as I listen to the sounds of my childhood—Mother's late night chats with Barbara, Jani in the bedroom shuffling her feet to jazz, my "chopsticks" on the piano, the banging of pots and pans—I suddenly remember skipping down the street with Mother, happy in my leggings, en route to my first haircut. We waited as the barber, finishing a wash-and-set, kept stealing glances at me. Finally he exclaimed, "What a magnetic personality!"

"She didn't even open up her mouth," objected Mother.

"She doesn't have to."

On the first anniversary of my father's death, Barbara was serving Mother breakfast, when I saw the memorial candle burning in the window. "What's that?" I asked.

"It's Daddy's birthday in heaven," Mother said. I walked to the window and sang, "Happy birthday to you," then turned, delighted to find them in tears. That night, on a rare visit to synagogue, I asked Mother, "Do you think, if we pray very hard, God will bring Daddy back?" and all but brought down the women's balcony.

If ever an actor's life was preordained, it was mine.

Chapter Two

*I*n first grade I shouted out whatever came into my mind at any given moment. I remember tall, skinny Miss Powers beating in rhythm with her stick at the blackboard, "One and one are two."

"Who told *you?*"

She'd stand me in the corner with a dunce cap on, or put me into the wastebasket under her desk. At year's end, she summoned my sister from her fifth grade studies and, pointing to me, inquired, "How does a thing like this emerge?" Head bowed, Jan shrugged her shoulders. "Well for two pins I'd leave her back!" The whole class laughed. I looked for the pins. I could be a comedian, too!

But, despite my efforts, I couldn't learn and was called stupid so often I believed it. Well, how was it possible *not* to believe when I tried so hard to listen? Seated in back with the tallest and fattest, I leaned forward the better to hear. Why that slight motion of my body should send my concentration flying, I don't know. But I do know that, in the process of trying to figure out certain taken-for-granted assumptions, I lost track of my teachers' next words. No sooner did I hear "All men are created equal" than I wondered, Equal to what?

I was fascinated by all their frowns and smiles. I had spent so much time in darkness, I literally drank them in. But so intent was my looking, I couldn't listen too. What was on my mind? What but the appetites of my body?

Every day I'd come straight home from school to find an older man masturbating under our stairwell. (Jani remembers him too.) Finally, I asked Mother, "Why is a man's wee-wee white?" and told her why I wanted to know.

"You mean you just stood there and watched him? You shouldn't do that," she chided. But I didn't think she was really listening to me. Anyway, she didn't give me any reason for her feeling. Daddies were nicer than mommies.

At age six, I went alone to the movies on weekends at the nearby Loews Delancey, which admitted children only if accompanied by an adult. Money in hand, I'd ask a stranger on line, "Could you please take me in?" Then I'd sit by myself and look at the faces around me. Everyone was quiet.

The first time a gentleman joined me and, hat in lap, exposed himself, my nerves flooded with familiar pleasure. This had happened somewhere before. He eyed me: would I go or stay? Then, covering us up with his coat, "Cross your leg over mine." Later: "You like candy? Be right back." I waited. He never returned. I'd wait for others. Alone, I felt tormented. The noise of words disturbed me. So I'd turn around in my seat: "Hey Mister, you want to play?"

Afterward I'd walk the narrow streets of East Broadway, catching strangers' eyes. I liked to make them look at me, make them stop and stare. To hawkers, bakers, big-bellied butchers in bloody aprons slapping their meat on the counters, "Interesting, isn't it?" I'd say. Sometimes I'd take rides on buses because they made me feel I was going somewhere. Christmas week I got off at Macy's, and finding Santa Claus on a break at the stocking counter, asked him confidentially, "Mister, aren't you hot with all those clothes on? Why don't you take your beard off?"

～

I was eight when Mother petitioned her neighboring jewelers on the Bowery to close early for the Friday night Sabbath. That she judged the religious weak, and God their necessary crutch, never stopped her from invoking the commandments for a good cause. But when she discovered that her competitors had decided amongst themselves, "If Ethel Hebald wants to take the Sabbath off, let her!" my courageous Mother fought back. Dropping in on them unannounced while her clerks minded the store, she took them on one by one:

"You dare to call yourselves gentlemen?" (They were *gentlefortzes*, Yiddish for "gentlefarts," behind their backs.) "Where's your honor? You have wives to care for your youngsters. My poor kids have no one!"

To us she said, "If God grants us this, we'll just hug Him and kiss Him all over." And she won! Not only Friday nights, but Saturday mornings, too, we'd have her all to ourselves. Well, Saturday mornings, anyway. The fact is, she'd fallen in love with a play-boy named Al.

"*Did* you?" asked twelve-year-old Jan. Mother nodded yes.

"Did you what?" I pressed, eager to join in the fun.

"You shouldn't ask me that," she balked modestly.

It was 1942. Shotgun marriages were booming with engagement ring sales—"Half price on the Bowery"—to boys going to war. Mother had earned enough to move us uptown directly across from Al on fashionable East Eighty-eighth Street. Friday nights, Jan and I would stretch out on Mother's bed and watch her dress for her date. Flesh tucked into her corset, her small breasts into her bra, she'd wiggle carefully into her dress, then pull it down. "Not too tight? Jani, zip me up." With a glance at her backward profile, she'd check her hem in the full-length mirror, then straighten her stocking seams. Stepping back for a fuller view, she'd sigh, "Beautiful. Just beautiful." Then, "I have two attractive daughters, but they don't hold a candle to me."

19

On the Friday nights Al didn't date her, she'd peer from her darkened bedroom into his living room. If the lights were on, he was home. If it was dark, there were two possibilities: he was out with one of his "whores," or he was peering into *her* room. "Keep it dark," she'd say. "Let him think we're out. If the phone rings, don't pick up."

Saturday mornings, Jan and I would creep into her bed. Who would we marry? asked Jan. Mother regarded us carefully. "Carol will marry a playboy," she decided. "And Jani? You'll marry an artist." Jani was heartbroken. Artists were ugly; playboys were handsome. If handsome loves beautiful, then like married like. Well, with her thick mop of curls thinned out and touched with Mother's henna rinse, she'd be beautiful, too.

I remember them arguing very excitedly one day about a pimple. I had an important question to ask "Don't interrupt!" They were growing more passionate by the minute.

"But I've been squeezing it and squeezing it!"

"Then stop it!"

I tried again. "Shut up!"

"Do you think my pimple will ever go 'way?" whined Jan.

"No!" announced Mother, triumphantly. Then to me, "Now, what is it you wanted to ask me?"

"I forgot."

"Again, forgot?"

Mother enrolled us in prestigious P.S. 6 on Madison Avenue. In third grade, but still unable to read, I was placed in the Sight-Conservation Class for slow learners, which served the offspring of the neighborhood poor. Unable to listen or learn, the only white girl there, I cried quietly and uncontrollably from my seat. Meanwhile, Jan had joined the Buddy Club, was talented in drawing, and was even getting pretty.

In hopes of bringing back a husband, Barbara returned to her native Hungary, and Mother hired a series of day maids. Among them was good, black Southern Queenie who complained in vain of Janice's cruelty to me. Perhaps our slave and master games, though fun for me sometimes, rubbed salt in the wounds of her own experience.

"Bring me the toilet," commanded Jani.

"I can't budge it, Your Majesty."

"Take ten lashes."

Sometimes we'd yelp with laughter. But if ever I refused to serve her, Janice banged my head repeatedly against the wall. "It's just not right!" argued Queenie to Mother the day she quit.

Not long after, when Barbara returned triumphant to reclaim her old job, it was Queenie's keen sense of justice that gave me courage to protest. Had Mother forgotten that Barbara had locked me in closets? (I'd told after she left.) Of course not! But didn't I agree that Barbara cooked the best chicken *paprikás?* Besides, Mother was her old confidante. And "the poor thing" had finally met someone. She'd sleep over at her sister's in Brooklyn and work for us weekdays only until she earned her fiancé's passage to the States.

Since we'd moved uptown, I spent weekend afternoons at the movies, ate supper afterward in the Automat, and, with Jan and Mom on dates, returned to an empty apartment. Now, to avoid Barbara, I also went to the movies every day after school. With a choice of four neighborhood theaters—Loews Eighty-sixth Street, Loews Third Avenue, RKO, and the Grande, I'd hop from one to the other. Grinning baldies bidding their Milky Ways along the children's section still found me sitting a little apart. The candy was for later.

One bleak Sunday afternoon I walked to Central Park, and

finding it deserted, curled up on the grass and fell asleep. I dreamed a strange man in a black coat was coming toward me. I made no effort to move, because I knew he'd take my hand and lead me to a lovely, wine-colored forest where we'd be warm. The man wouldn't look at me. The stare in his eye was wild and lonely. The touch of his hand was cold. Soon we arrived at a warm spot enclosed by a great cluster of red and black leaves. A heavy summer rain began to fall, but our circle was warm and dry. He sat on a tree stump and pulled me to his lap. I turned to put my arms around his neck, but he took me across his knee and spanked me hard. I wanted to turn around, to throw my arms about his neck once again, but I was afraid he'd let me fall, so I held tightly to his knees as the blood rushed to my head and I started to scream.

~

Weeknights, as soon as Jan finished her homework she'd order me to entertain her. This I loved. I'd climb up on the dresser, her best view of me from bed, and my feet tapping in rhythm, my arms plowing the air, I'd dance and sing for her. From Mother she demanded new clothes. "You can afford to be generous," she gibed. "All my friends have birthday parties, they celebrate holidays. What do we celebrate? Not even Thanksgiving!"

I'd lug her books to and from the Ninety-sixth Street Library, then watch her read, hour after hour.

"Jani?"

"What?"

"Talk to me."

"Not now!" Immersed in Nancy Drew, she'd brook no interruptions. For spite I opened a book! Fixing my eyes on every word, the spaces above, below, and between, I imagined the sense would come to me. A hundred times my eyes ran over the same sentence. I had mastered the alphabet but couldn't connect the letters to make words. And so I tried again. And again and again and again until I did what Jani did, banged my head repeatedly against the wall.

Is it possible to describe how tormented the mind becomes when it cannot learn? A mind, an ordinary mind, that can't pause long enough to consider the probable consequences of two actions, for example, to interrupt Jani or to leave, will pose a hundred other possibilities, slip into fantasy, and stand absolutely still. Now consider a not-so-ordinary mind, then triple the ratio of actions to possibilities, pretzeling into knots and finally choking for lack of air. I was in the closet again; I couldn't breathe.

One fine day, I asserted myself: "If you don't teach me how to read, I'll never be your slave again."

"What'll you give me?" asked Jan.

"Anything."

And good Jani *did* teach me, that spring in Central Park, first to sound out the words. "C-A-T—say it." She showed me a picture: "This is a C-A-T. CAT. Say it. Repeat it. Say it again."

The following year I was put into a regular class.

But everyone knew where I came from. We were learning the names and populations of the states in Mrs. Martin's fourth grade class, and had just reached Virginia when little Richard Webster behind me tapped my shoulder and whispered in my ear: "You are *not* the first six letters of that state's name."

"That's right!" I snarled.

"Hebald, buckle your tongue," commanded Mrs. Martin. Instead, I stuck it out. "How *dare* you? Class, how *dare* she?"

Later a group of them chased me home from school, cornered me against a building, and took turns hitting me over the head with their briefcases. That evening, Mother rose to answer the doorbell.

"Please excuse us, I tried you earlier," came the cultured voice of our upstairs neighbor. With her was one of the girls who had chased me. "This is my daughter, Ada. She has something to say to Carol."

Pale Ada, avoiding my eyes, confessed: "I . . . some other girls too . . . we beat up Carol today."

"I think it's terrible that a daughter of mine could mistreat a child without a father," said the woman with feeling.

Mother burst into tears. "I didn't know. Carol didn't tell me."

Ada, forced to apologize, stuck out a limp hand, which I shook at her mother's bidding.

"There was murder in that child's eyes," said Mother after they'd left. But I didn't see murder, only chagrin and shame. "Never mind," she went on. "They're jealous of you! Just you wait and see. My poor child, so neglected." If I were a cat, I'd have purred. Our tears were painful, delicious. I savored them.

No one liked me at Camp Guilford that summer, either—not until I had my first triumph: cast in a weekend musical performance, I sang and danced with such naive and wholehearted faith in the fictions around me, I was rewarded by total audience attention. Jan came back with her bunkmates, all crying, "Bravo! You were wonderful!"

My counselors agreed. "Be that good tomorrow night."

"Well I might, and I might not," I replied, feeling a bit of power. This stopped them in their tracks. Then, "I'd like a zombie," I announced coolly. I'd learned of this popular alcoholic drink from my sister, who probably heard of it on the street. Now they were on me like flies on sugar: "Where did you learn that word? Aw come on, tell us." I wouldn't.

Nor did I disappoint them next evening on stage, but for a solid week after, I refused to eat or play games. When even Jan couldn't persuade me to "shape up," Mother was summoned for an emergency visit. Did I want to get sick? No, I wanted to be cared for. But if getting sick was what it took . . . ? Or had the recent attention I'd tasted inflamed my need for more? Oh, much, much more!

I suppose after Mother left I began to eat a little. But I went to activities only to watch, and refused to join in my bunkmates' bedtime talks: Pimples, dimples, who had what, and who wanted it—is that all life was about? Yes, I had begun to listen. Something indeed was happening.

~

That fall, Al rejected Mother cruelly. She'd taken all day Saturday off to be with him. I begged to come along. The three of us were standing on a windy Coney Island pier, when Mother broached the subject of marriage.

"I wouldn't marry you if you were the last woman on earth," said original Al. Mother stared at the ocean. A strong wind untied the loose knot of her purple silk scarf, which flew from her neck into the waves. "Do you think we can get it back?" she asked, suddenly a tender child.

Her affair over, Mother moved us to a larger, cheaper apartment on East Eighty-fourth Street, where, to keep peace with Jan, I slept in the little maid's room off the kitchen. When Barbara's fiancé finally arrived from Hungary, she was replaced by gentle, Polish Pauline, a music lover who sighed deeply whenever I practiced the piano. Jan could play Chopin. And I? "What D'ya Do in the Infantry? Ya march, Ya march, Ya march."

One day, when Pauline was at the market:

"I can't play it," I told the teacher.

"Count it out then. Can't you count?" she asked me gently. I tried to answer, but I couldn't. A hard lump lodged in my throat;

25

my eyes rested on her prominent wrist bone, the soft hair on her arm. I rose and went back to my room. Jan was called to the piano.

"Hair and fabrics ignite instantly" had been the lesson that day at school. But *how* instant is "instantly"? I wondered, lighting a match to the kitchen curtains. "Excuse me for interrupting," I said. The three of us put out the fire.

I wouldn't admit what I'd done. I said the wind blew the curtain onto the gas jet. Pauline shook her head. Yes, dinner *was* cooking on a low flame, but the curtain ends had been tacked to the wall. What's more, they hadn't been touched. Nobody punished me for lying. It was simply expected of me.

I was ten when petite, polite Debby, the popular new girl from around the corner, introduced me to Judy and Madge. One day after school the four of us had gathered at Judy's. "My mother bought me the most disgusting coat," she crabbed in the way proper girls drew attention to their clothes.

"I have a new coat too," I said. "D'ya like it?"

"Not really," they agreed. "It's brown."

"But it looks nice on you," added Debby.

Now, in the interest of improving ourselves, Madge suggested we confess our true feelings about one another. "Judy, you're very nice, except stop slouching." "Madge should start brushing her teeth. Girls with green teeth don't rate." As for Debby, "Except for your braces, hubba-hubba" (slang for wow!).

"What about me?"

The general consensus was: "We all feel sorry for you."

"They're just jealous," scoffed Jan that evening.

Well, which was it? Did my family lie to me from pity? Or had my "jealous" friends told the truth?

By 1944 I'd been reading for a solid year. With the developing news of the war, and D day fast approaching, I was learning new words so quickly that I often made mistakes. I thought *blitz* meant bomb, and *bomb,* airplane. So when bulky, belligerent Mrs. Martin remarked at school how grateful we should be that never in American history had we experienced an air raid, I yelled out: "There was a bomb over *my* house last night."

"Shut it!"

"It's true, it's true," I protested.

"Shut it," she warned, "or CHARGE in the section book!"

"A double demerit? But, but . . ."

"But, but? A word to the wise is sufficient."

"Then listen!" I cried out.

"CHARGE!" she shouted like Theodore Roosevelt.

"Okay, charge me—but I saw it, I heard it. The noise—it was awful! Oh, terrible," I shuddered.

The bell rang. "Carol, come here," she said. Then, seriously, "Where do you live?" she demanded, as though it were just possible I commuted to school every day from Europe! I learned my verbal error soon enough. But I learned also the first law of acting: believe, and you'll be believed. I had the gift and knew it. So when, a few days later, Mrs. Martin quoted Lincoln's famous words, "You can fool some of the people all of the time, and all of the people some of the time, but you can't fool all of the people all of the time," I shouted out, "*I* can!"

When I was promoted, "It's because I couldn't stand to have you twice," said fat, fatuous old Mrs. Martin whose sudden death that summer convinced me that God was in heaven.

I found further proof of His existence in Mrs. Kessler, who called on me the following term to give an extemporaneous talk. I rose and announced my subject: "My Imaginary Forest: A Recitation from My Mind." In it was a tree—"my tree," I called it. Climbing it, I saw a great kingdom that I started to describe, when my classmates' embarrassed giggles sent me back to my seat.

"I'm very disappointed in you," said sharp, loving Mrs. Kessler, who often kept me in. Sitting upright at her desk, correcting papers, she'd let me empty the trash or wash the blackboard. Then she'd talk to me a while. Did my mother read me fairy tales about forests?

"Never," I told her. "We don't believe in fairy tales."

"No? What does your father do?"

"He's dead," I said.

"Do you remember him?" she asked me kindly.

"No." I'd forgotten him entirely.

I continued to get D's in conduct. But the evaluations on my report card changed that year from "is doing very poor work" to "could do better." No longer was I in danger of being left back.

On weekends, my sexual delights at the movies were followed by gastronomical ones at the Eighty-sixth Street Automat: beef pot pies for thirty cents, pie and ice cream for a quarter, milk for a nickel. Then I'd come home and enter my fantasies.

I'd switch on the radio, slip into my mother's high heels, and perform in front of her mirror. Through my renditions of "Pistol Packin' Mama," "If You Are But a Dream," "Paper Doll," "Long Ago and Far Away," a huge audience sat rapt in wonder:

"Look at her! She moves like an angel!"

"Shhhh . . . watch!"

The year was 1945. I was eleven. Movie moguls were distracting the American public from the war with lavish musicals like *Thank Your Lucky Stars* and *Get Hep to Jazz*. Between newsreels and full-length features came the "short subjects." One remains fixed in my mind: an attractive woman, hailing a cab outside an elegant department store, held a package in her other hand. "This lady has just bought a new dress," observed the narrator. "She boasts of a new dress every two weeks. But with few, if any friends, she has little chance to wear them. Ladies and gentlemen, we see before us a single woman—successful, self-centered, and lonely." His voice grew tremulous.

But whoever portrayed this woman played wisely *against* her loneliness. She was tall, she had dignity; I was she. Yes, I was glimpsing my future. Why otherwise should I remember it? Something special was in store, and I knew it.

I knew also that certain injuries had been done to me from which I never would heal.

Chapter Three

At eleven years old, I walked out of a musical film at the Grande Theater and had my first revelation from God. I heard no astral melody, no angel descended on a cloud. Just an unearthly voice, bell toned and clear, echoing in a radiance of light, "You will be a great actress."

In an instant I knew all I had lived through was ordained and that I must have faith in the future. It was early spring. I ran from sheer joy all around Central Park. Fresh air filled my lungs with the literal impulse to fly. I saw a wildly happy bird, flitting this way and that, tear its way through a cloud. I couldn't resist calling after it. "Hey, crazy kid," some man hollered.

Landing home, I found Mother at the bathroom mirror dolling up for a date with her fiancé, elegant, Russian-born Sam Morrison. Upright, bald, with a patrician forehead and wide-slung eyes, Sam manufactured ladies' cosmetic compacts in New Brunswick. During the war his profits had soared, thanks to government contracts to produce metal good for ammunition. He drove proudly to work in a spiffy maroon Buick. Mother was in an excellent mood. After nine years behind the counter, she'd finally sold the store.

The whole upheaval of circumstances disturbed me deeply. Accustomed to my orphan status, I'd begun to take a certain pride in it and didn't want parents thrust upon me—not these, and not now. Sam I hardly knew. But Mother, who'd long since become a stranger to me, had so entirely changed with her coming status as Upper East Side homemaker. I didn't know how to respond when she'd imitate the speech and mannerisms of her upscale neighbors: "Shut up or I'll break every bone in your body" became "If you don't behave, I'll spank you." Spank me?

She was penciling her brows at the bathroom mirror when I burst in on her that day from the park. "I'm going to be an actress. Mother, please—I have to. Cancel my piano lessons! Let me study dramatics instead. Please."

She paused in surprise. Finally, "I think it would be nice for a daughter of mine to have *elocution* lessons."

"No, Mother—please. *You* take elocution. Let me have dramatics."

She'd think about it. That Monday after school, I went to the Drama Bookshop and bought Stanislavsky's *An Actor Prepares*. From it I learned that acting is an art, and experience the artist's hunting ground; that for us suffering is neither random nor meaningless so long as we can put it to use. Yes, the harm of early hurt had a purpose. There was reason now to bear everything, even to ask for more. From my little maid's room window I prayed nightly for a torture of yearning, to be nourished by the whole gamut of human experience—including insanity itself—to help me recreate on the stage all states of being firsthand. I experienced a great silence and solemnity. No longer a discipline problem at school, I barely spoke; I did my work.

I was twelve and a half when Mother enrolled me in an acting class at the Ninety-second Street Y, where I met my first real friend. Merna, at fourteen, weighed an unfashionable 130 and lived in the friendly Bronx. To me she was immensely attractive: a soft, maternal voice, an oval face, a short and sturdy build. She passed easily for eighteen. One Sunday afternoon, dressed in high heels and makeup, we tottered into Tavern on the Green and ordered our first martinis. Mine tasted like rancid perfume. Drunk, puffing on cigarettes "to dilute it," we told each other everything: she'd already menstruated, had I? Just last month! When my step-father heard the news, he'd smacked me hard across the face. "An old Russian custom," he explained, "to show it's no laughing matter." I hadn't thought it was. "Maybe he feels anxious because you're pretty," suggested Merna mysteriously.

She was a good, conscientious student from a poor and troubled family—all the women in it were "nervous," all had doctors. Merna urged me to find one, too. She'd be a writer, I, an actress. She found life "terribly painful." Pain was our favorite word. "I see an awful lot of pain in your face, Carol." I told her I wasn't the best actress in the class, but could be. "What about you as a person?" she asked. "Being a person isn't important," I answered.

Soon my weekly acting classes at the Y were not enough. I wanted individual instruction. In April of my senior year at P.S. 6, I auditioned in Mother's presence for the private coach Joseph Geiger.

When I was done: "How old are you?" asked the bald, kind-faced old gentleman.

"She'll be thirteen in July," answered Mother.

"She has a beautiful talent," he told her.

Weeks later, Geiger gathered his advanced private students together to practice sight-reading skills. I was asked to read Lisa from Maxwell Anderson's *High Tor*. It was agreed I'd given a brilliant performance. How did I feel? Comfortable, that's all. Lisa was so close to me, I simply stepped into her skin. But that I could reach such heights without having preread the text? I kept silent. This was sacred proof God had kept His word: I would be a great actress.

Little did I realize that my "performance" was nothing more

than an inspired accident. My later homework on the part proved futile. Nothing could wake up my will. But the actor *creates* at will; he sheds his daily cares with his outside clothing. How otherwise begin? I had much to learn, so much! The road was long, the wrong turns many—how many! And practice makes worse if one works the wrong way. But work I did, blindly, at random, like a lunatic. If there was a difference between self-torture and self-discipline, I didn't know it. Nor, given the trouble I was headed for, could any teacher have told me. I was so at the mercy of their praise I learned nothing at all from them.

I had myself in a stranglehold. My work was much too important. The more I failed, the tenser I became. I feared I was losing my talent. Despair was taking over; like a wave flowing backwards I couldn't control its course. In the midst of a tender love scene, the words *fuck, shit, cunt* would sail into my mind as though for the sole purpose of locking me up.

Why? I was dreadfully ashamed of my body. My voluptuous, too-well-proportioned body! Passing me on the subway, some pimply faced kid snickered, "What are you? A 32C?" Men who'd long since stopped touching me in the movies now followed me on the street with their eyes. Was I ashamed of my hunger for them? Why should I be? I had healthy appetites. There was nothing the matter with that. Hadn't I heard Mother tell sixteen-year-old Jan: "The woman is supposed to purr to let the man know he's okay"? When turning to me she inquired, "Are you troubled by s-e-x?" "Maybe," I shrugged. "Then why don't you abuse yourself?" she suggested.

What other family was so open? Well aware mine was different, I didn't think us wrong for being so. But we were strange in some ways. When her mother slapped her face, Merna would just stand there and take it. But when Mother hit Jan, she hit back. I'd watch them wrestling on the floor like tigers, so ugly in their wretchedness, those rotten, shrieking voices! I'd slam the door on them. When they came after me with that bestial rage peculiar to the scorned, I'd imagine a gentle light in their eyes. I saw in all cruelty a tiny spark of mercy; I saw what I had to see. But I was in fantasy most of the time.

On solitary walks through streets and parks, I now read in the eyes of strangers a careful understanding of myself. Had someone sane, calm, wise, and strong then told me that just as clenched teeth help us bear intense physical pain, my muscular tension kept at bay intolerable psychic pain, would I have found courage to confront it?

One evening Geiger telephoned Mother. "She's the greatest student I've ever had, but take that child to a psychiatrist," he warned. What was the trouble? I hadn't played well that day. In the middle of my monologue from *St. Joan,* tension had crept into my body. Unable to follow a simple impulse to move, I froze, leaning forward. "Like the leaning tower of Pisa," he'd said, aping my awkward posture. His words were blades in my flesh. But I thought wrongly he'd hurt me on purpose. Certainly there are people whose mission in life is to kill in others what they lack in themselves, but Geiger wasn't one of them.

"She's so sensitive, it frightens me," he told Mother.

"She'll outgrow it," was her answer. "Just a little *clipkey in cup,*" which translates roughly from the Yiddish into a "little clothespin on her brain."

Next morning at the table: "You are a human being and not a machine, do you understand? You're supposed to have ups and downs."

"Yes, Mother. Thank you."

"Well, I enjoyed my breakfast very much," she said, rising regally. She wouldn't take me to a doctor. "But you haven't touched your food."

Nor would I. Lately, I'd been gaining weight. Maybe I was ashamed of my body because it was getting fat! No more sweets or starches. I bound my breasts tightly and dressed in boyish clothes. I'd masturbate until, but not including, climax. That ecstasy I'd save for my work. It mustn't be frittered away! Already, I felt the intimate relationship between sex and art by the way the former filters through certain passages in the Beethoven quartets that carry me to this day into heavenly spheres.

Onstage I wanted to touch the borders of feeling such music can express. For it was music I felt most deeply. At bedtime I'd turn on WQXR and let it play through my sleep on the chance that the geniuses of Bach, Beethoven, Mozart, and Schubert would seep into my soul. At first I felt confused by some of their more difficult chamber pieces, but made myself listen over and over until I was able to understand and therefore love them.

Still, tension continued to plague me. One day I confessed to Merna that I longed to scream out of my system all that was clogging it.

"A mental hospital is the place for that," she said.

A haven for the release of intolerable feelings? Really? Is that what those hospitals are for?

&

At seventeen, Jan's active interest in politics and history led her to explore the liberal publication *The Free Thinker*. "The Free Stinker," sneered Sam. Jan despised our stepfather. A divorced man, he wouldn't adopt us, yet felt duty bound to judge us. About personal matters he and Jan quarreled openly. But their arguments about America in time of war, the Truman presidency, Communism, Judaism, and the *goyish* problem piqued my inter-

est. For according to Sam, all non-Jews were jealous of our re-
markable success as a people. Success was money—that was that.
I hated his small-minded arrogance, but wanted a father, too.

One day I asked him to watch me play a monologue from *St.
Joan.* Self-conscious the first time, I tried again. That night I
heard him tell Mother, "She was better the second time." Mother
replied with a shrug in her voice, "I don't know; everything she
does stinks to me."

For her birthday that November I bought Mother a blue silk
handkerchief. She thanked me politely, then, when she thought I
was out of earshot, muttered to Sam, "Some cheap thing." But the
handkerchief I'd chosen was beautiful. I'd wanted so very much
to please her and searched long and hard to find a good imita-
tion lace, the most delicate shade of light blue. She never knew I
heard her. My agony was immense. Agony? Then how come,
catching sight of my face in the hall mirror just after, I thought,
"God, that's moving—remember it!"

Now I began to note everything Mother did with a falcon eye,
and came to judge her as mercilessly in silence as she judged me
in words. I wouldn't forgive her. Nor did I bother to consider
what lay behind her special cruelty. Who was she? What little girl
had she been? More than the excellent student forced to drop out
of school, more than the sum of all her disappointments. I once
asked her what she dreamed of as a child. "A bathtub and a man
with a car," she said. But now she had much more than that. Why
was it that the more she had, the unhappier she became?

☙

In fall 1947, "The Best Things in Life Are Free" was the song on
everyone's lips. I was thirteen when *Miss America* Magazine told
girls my age how to rate boys: Do you flatter him? He needs it.
Are you truly feminine? How much do you weigh? Do you feel

less than perky on those certain days of the month? Don't lie in bed with your lily. Freshen up and go! What's your usual scent? He may *say* he likes that soap-and-water freshness, but does he mean it? Do *you* always mean what you say? Oh, you foolish girl! Smile! And don't forget that daily bath, that touch of Tangee lipstick (Don't blot. Boys like lips that shine!), and a neat, clean purse, because a messy purse *might* be his pet peeve. And since nobody likes a fat girl, nurse your Cokes and pretzels because, let's face it, a girl who doesn't eat is a creep.

Normal teenagers only dreamed of such futures as mine. Lectured on the pitfalls of immature values, their conversations circled around what "a clever girl" did or didn't do to achieve her clever goals. Meanwhile, seventeen-year-old Jan had fallen for a handsome ne'er-do-well named Danny, roughly twelve years her senior. "He has no job, no ambition," balked Mother, who rallied Sam to include Jan on a weekend jaunt to a Lakewood, New Jersey, resort, "where maybe she'll meet someone else." I tagged along.

No sooner had we arrived than a cub of twenty introduced himself to Jan: "Greetings! I'm Bernie." Within the hour they were fighting. She called him a pseudointellectual; he called her bourgeois. That night, entertaining some guests around the fireplace with a recital of "My Imaginary Forest," I saw tall, lean Bernie listening in the doorway. When I was done, he took me aside. "You're obviously an artist," he began, pouring his brown saucer eyes into mine. "I'm going to be an actress," I replied. "Oh? Just don't be a prostitute with your imagination," he quipped, and walked away.

I followed. His words were freighted with meaning . . . exactly what? I was not to squander my gifts, he said. My interest was instantly aroused. Who was this gaunt, thin-legged young man

whose huge eyes pierced me like suns? An English major and
would-be writer from Rutgers University. Would I meet him next
Saturday in New York? "Eat home," he advised, "because I'm
poor."

Walking through Central Park, we found a special tree—Our
Tree we came to call it—under which we made love. It was a
painful, quick, unpleasant business. Afterward, "You weren't a
virgin," he remarked, and demanded to know why. I didn't *know*
why, or why he should have cared. He didn't seem to love me.
When, in one of his weekly letters, he called me a "fey-like crea-
ture whose imagination warms me with a kinship to it," I assumed he was practicing composition. He wrote of drifting from
movie to movie on lonely nights, "sleepless, tormented—and
probably insane."

It struck me years later that like Merna and me, Bernie cher-
ished his pain but alone claimed the distinction of insanity, his
many protestations of it offset only by his healthy appetites for
social status and sex. One weekend I had my period and dared
refuse him the latter. "But I came in from New Jersey! I'm making the supreme sacrifice. Please let me know the next time you
decide to menstruate."

He could be arrested for statutory rape so I should keep my
mouth shut. Then, after boasting of his prowess to his peers, he
reported their responses to me: "How's little Carol? Does her
mama know?" I didn't object. In fact, I was pleased.

"You're so quiet," he observed one day. And when I made no
answer, "In case you're thinking of marrying me, I have heart disease."

"That's okay," I said, "so do I."

"Aren't you ever going to talk to me?" he complained. "Other
girls talk my ear off."

"What should I say?"

"What's on your mind!"

When I tried: "That's fallacious," he'd reply.

A strange incident followed. Merna had bought me a scarf for Christmas that I was eager to show to Sam. "Isn't it beautiful?" I asked.

"Never mind beautiful," he scoffed. "How much did it cost?"

I was still brooding over this petty slight when, a night or so later, Sam returned from an evening out with Mother, and peered into my maid's room to ask, as was his habit, "You okay, kid?"

"Yes, thanks."

On his way to the master bedroom he collapsed.

"Sam?" Mother called out. His glazed eyes fixed open, he couldn't move or speak. In one blow, he'd suffered a heart attack and stroke.

But the sequence of events was much too close! Years before, I had imagined that God killed Mrs. Martin for her cruelty to me; was He punishing Sam for the same reason? Mother, ever dry-eyed and clear minded in a crisis, asked me to get the "super" to help us drag him onto the bed before phoning for an ambulance. His head fell back when we lifted him, and the whole of his body was inert. His hands were deadly pale. One looked stiff and mis-shapen; wiry gray hairs sprouted above the knuckles. I took it, then let it fall at his side.

Weeks later, Sam left the hospital for the Institute for Rehabilitation, where, paralyzed on the left side of his face and body, his speech badly impaired, he completed his physical therapy. The day we took him home, Mother wheeled him outside to the taxi stand. "How such a thing can happen to a man," he said, his shoulders shaking with sobs.

"No. No self-pity," she chided, not unkindly.

Never a religious man, he now summoned Christian Science faith healers to the house. When one accused him of choosing his illness, he returned to the Judaism of his birth and prayed all day at his bedroom window. Never one to pamper, Mother insisted he wheel himself to the dining room for meals. Eventually, he was able to circle the block on crutches to attend daily services at the neighborhood synagogue.

Chapter Four

I was to graduate from P.S. 6 in June 1948. The following September, the artistic division of Metropolitan Vocational High School, in lower Manhattan, would move up to the Broadway theater district and become the School of Performing Arts. Spring auditions were held for budding actors, dancers, and musicians. Asked to prepare two three to five minute sketches, I chose a monologue from *St. Joan* and "My Imaginary Forest." This latter piece caught the attention of a guest judge, the Broadway producer Brock Pemberton.

"Did you write that yourself?" he asked when I was done.

"It's an improvisation," I answered. "I go to a forest in my mind and just say what I see."

He rose, and with an important air, declared to the other judges, "She's a writer! We need writers, not actors!"

Excused, I returned to the waiting room for my coat, when the secretary, sent to summon the one other P.S. 6 applicant, caught my eye and mouthed reverently, "You passed!"

A day or so later, a reporter from the *New York Sunday Mirror Magazine* phoned. He'd heard about my audition and was writing an essay on the school. Was I planning to attend? I was! Then would I pose for a cover photo? Yes! I screamed. I was thrilled. Shortly before it came out, Mrs. Kessler, letter in hand from Performing Arts, ran triumphantly down the corridors, interrupting classes to announce, "Valerie and Carol got in! Val passed with two 'fairs' and three 'goods,' but Carol Hebald got 'outstanding' in all five categories—talent, speech, deportment, poise, and appearance!"

Wonderful Mrs. Kessler. Bless you, wherever you are. I'm ashamed to think how many years went by before I remembered her kindness. Or how many more before I'd recall my father's last words to me: "Be somebody." Troubled children seldom believe the reminder that there were good things, too, until we've survived the bad. But we had to find strength somewhere to bear the suffering, didn't we?

A few weeks before graduation Mother, examining my cover-page photo, commented to Sam in the kitchen: "I don't know whether she's laughing or crying."

"*She's* sitting right here," I reminded her.

"So what if she has a little talent."

"A little?" I was outraged.

The phone rang. Jumping up to answer it, I overturned a glass of milk. "Why?" screamed Mother. "Why do you torment me?"

"I'm sorry! Isn't that enough?"

But as though I'd done it on purpose: "No, it's not enough! Not enough!"

All that day Jan was expecting a call from Danny; when the phone rang again, it was for me. I got off fast, only to hear from the kitchen Jan's loud whine to Mother: "But he promised to call! Danny's a bullshit artist!"

"That's right!"

There was a clanking of coffee cups in the sink.

"Carol is a bullshit artist," added Jan.

"I know," sighed Mother disconsolately.

But Danny did call, and that June he married my sister.

Now with Sam on his back and Jan gone, I'd walk with Mother on a Sunday and watch her avert her eyes from couples going happily about. She had no friends and wanted them least of all now. At the hurting pity of a neighbor's gaze, "What is *she* looking at?" she'd mutter. To whom but me could she confess that Sam wouldn't have sex because he feared an orgasm would kill him? "You think I don't have desires?"

"Why don't you call your sister Fanny?" I suggested.

"What's Fanny to me?" she snapped, or any other jealous sibling who'd bless her heart and stab her in the back? No; with her own mother ailing, to me alone could she grieve over Jan: "Danny moves her to *his* parents' house and tells *her* to get a job!" She couldn't keep quiet, even with Beethoven playing on the Victrola. Rehearsing her misery at the "sad parts," "*Why?*" she wailed, "Why am I so cursed?" When I left the room, "Where are you going?" she shrilled after me. "Why do you run away?"

How tell her simply and with grace that I couldn't bear her misery any better than she could mine? "Because I don't like you," I answered finally.

"You don't like me," she echoed, the tears springing to her eyes. I knew in a flash she'd heard it before, and never forgave myself for saying it. She refused to attend my graduation. She'd never had one of her own.

That July I turned fourteen. With nothing to do on my birthday, I got dressed after breakfast. "Where are you going?" she asked.

"To the movies."

"Again to the movies, always to the movies." And, too unhappy to know what she was doing, she wrestled me to the floor and hit me. "I'll cripple you," she kept repeating, "I'll cripple you." I ran into the bathroom.

"Why? For what? Are you crazy?" I screamed behind the door.

Later that summer, finding a wallet in Central Park, I phoned its grateful owner, who offered me a reward. Refusing it, I arranged a time for him to come and pick it up.

When Mother raised her hand to me again: "Not everybody would do that!" I was a fool not to take what I could get, was that it? Even if I didn't need it?

At night I'd sneak into the kitchen and eat till I could eat no more. Drifting into dreams, I'd sleep like a statue until morning. That summer I gained ten pounds and bought myself a fully boned corset I never left home without.

In August I asked again to see a psychiatrist. "I suffer, too," I told Mother. I wanted some sign, some token from her, that she knew. "You don't know what suffering is!" she taunted. Hers outranked the world's.

"I'm afraid I'll tense up again at school," I told her.

"Then go to a regular high school."

"Oh, no!"

"What can a doctor do for you that I can't?"

~

On the first day of school, I was in for a shock. The *Mirror Magazine* reporter had wisecracked in his essay, "High School for Hams," that Performing Arts was the perfect place "for all the oddballs to gather under one roof." No sooner was I seated in Mrs. Provet's homeroom class than the others accused me of feeding him that line. It was useless to deny it; I wasn't believed.

From day one, I fought with my teachers about Stanislavsky. I had nothing to fight *about;* I just wanted them to know I'd read him. Then couldn't I have told them so? Not without seeming to curry favor. But a few weeks into the semester, I earned the attention I craved during an exercise in emotional recall. When I had reclaimed my seat, "Do you always cry like that?" asked drama department chair, Dr. Dycke.

"Yes, everybody does," I answered.

"No, not everybody," she returned solemnly.

I fell instantly in love, and from that day forward would listen through morning academics for her quick footstep down the hall. When she'd spot me at change of classes, she'd approach me briskly. "How are you, my pet?" she'd ask, scanning me from head to toe. Then, "You need earrings with that short haircut, but the color of your blouse is good."

At midterm I brought home my report card. Though I'd done well in acting and dance, I was unhappy over my academic C's.

"What do you care?" asked Mother. "All you want is to pass."

Is that all she thought I wanted? Or all she wanted me to want? Now that I knew where I stood with her, I began to do better for spite.

~

Relations with Bernie had been unpleasant from the start. With the onset of winter—our tree in Central Park bare, our nesting ground covered with snow—I resolved to end them. But how? Demand a platonic interlude? Or plead the truth: at fourteen sex made me guilty. It was from Dr. Dycke I wanted advice; but as Mrs. Provet's "homeroomer," I had no choice.

"What would you say if I told you I was having an affair?" I asked Mrs. Provet off the bat at my conference.

"An affair with . . . ?"

"A college man."

"I'd say you should stop it right away!" she blustered. "How long has this been going on?"

"Since last spring. I want to stop it, but I don't know how!" I lied.

"Why not ask his intentions? Ask him if he's planning to marry you."

And like a good girl, I did. "Get it out of your mind," he said.

It wasn't difficult. The relationship cooled quickly to a stop.

Mrs. Provet had told Dr. Dycke, as I hoped and prayed she would. Will I ever forget my delight at their whispers and sidelong glances at me during assembly?

"Do you think Dr. Dycke likes me?" I'd asked Merna, whom I met on Fridays after school in Greenwich Village. We'd follow people who looked "literary," or watch some girls making plastic flowers in a dirty factory near Bleecker Street. At six o'clock the tall office buildings closed for the weekend. The Italian restaurants that lined the streets gushed out odors of vegetable incense as we passed. And the crowds, the cars, the machines made us long for a retreat without a litter of broken bottles and crushed eggshells. Heading east, the sightseeing buses groaned. And the lesbian-gay bars were full to bursting with straight women who'd gotten "raw deals." Outside, tourists sat about on fire hydrants dashing off souvenir postcards. "Howdy!" we'd salute, and go in.

Oh, it was fun being juvenile delinquents, dancing in butch clothing for the New York University psych majors who came in pairs to observe the "queers." Stephanie Stunnings and Charley Convertibles, we called them. We were just playing, weren't we? Merna had a Saturday night boyfriend. How about me? When I told her the idea of being gay intrigued me, she urged me again to seek help. Did I know about the new, low-cost outpatient clinic at Manhattan's Mount Sinai Hospital that was free for poor kids, provided they had their parents' consent? "My mother isn't poor," I reminded her, "she just won't consent."

"Then keep after her," advised my friend.

And so I did, at the start of my sophomore year, when Jan had separated from Danny and moved back home with us. "Tell them you live with Grandma in the Bronx," sighed Mother at last. "That way they won't charge us."

Running the half mile home after my battery of psychological tests, I found her peeling potatoes at the sink. "Well?"

"They said I need a mother," I panted, all out of breath.

"In other words, I'm no good."

"That's right: you're no good!"

My sister yelped with laughter. Then all three of us howled.

~

At Mount Sinai, two white-coated men sat opposite me in a small room: brusque, young, poker-faced Dr. Adelson with a clipboard on his knee, and fatherly, soft-spoken Dr. King, who I hoped fervently would treat me.

"What brings you here today?" asked the latter with a smile.

"Just a question. Can great actors be homosexual?"

"Depends what you mean by *great*."

"Well," I considered. "Charles Laughton?"

"*I* think he fits the bill," said Dr. King. "Why do you ask?"

I paused, looking at his shoes, which seemed suddenly as big as canoes. "I'm afraid I'm becoming one," I admitted finally. "And I feel guilty because it's interfering with my work. Not only that. I can't concentrate."

"Concentrate where? In school?"

"In school, in the movies. I can't listen. I can't follow a simple story."

"What preoccupies you?"

"I don't know!"

"You're listening now."

"Because the discussion's about me."

Young Dr. Adelson laughed, turning a plump, sleek, bird-of-prey profile.

"Why don't you tell us about yourself?" urged his gracious elder. "Tell us a little about your life."

47

I began with my passion to act. Very early, I knew my life would be a vehicle to this end; my relationships, tools to serve it. I knew I'd never find happiness. Happiness was not my goal. When I'd finished, Dr. King remarked that it was most unusual for a girl of fourteen to feel that way.

"It's not that without acting I'm nothing," I explained. "It's just, without it I can't let myself have anything else."

Was that my most pressing complaint?

"That's not a complaint!" I exclaimed. "It's something else. Something's stifling me. I have to uncork it."

Head buried in his clipboard, Dr. Adelson took notes as I relayed my early experiences in the movies. Craning his pink neck above his collar, he assiduously avoided my eyes as Dr. King pressed me for details on who did what to whom. Acutely embarrassed, I searched for the words. "You know," I said finally, "with the finger."

"Oh, mutual masturbation!" boomed Dr. King. I sat there rigid with shame.

At the end of our interview, Dr. King asked if I was aware that I'd been smiling all through it. "No." The lie popped out so quickly. Only later would I recall that my father was described as "always smiling."

I was disappointed to learn I'd be working with Dr. Adelson. Although it was common knowledge that psychiatrists assumed poker faces onto which patients might "project" their problems, I found Adelson's stony stance an affront. His repeated question, "Why were you locked in closets?" contained the certain accusation that I'd deserved it. Pen always at the ready, he continued pecking away: "Do you know what an orgasm is?"

"Yes."

"Have you ever had one?"

"I've had many." I blew a smoke ring into the air.

"You know the difference between the clitoral and vaginal kinds?"

"Yes. Why?" I shot back. Again stretching his pink neck from his collar, he rolled his eyes up and away: What next?

"What are your other pleasures?" he asked, thin lips curled in distaste.

"Aside from food? Music." I answered coolly.

"What music? Whose?"

"Beethoven's in particular. Then Bach's, Mozart's, Schubert's."

"And do you find their music . . . sad?"

"Sad? Oh, no!" I exclaimed, and because I saw where he was trying to lead me, added quickly, "I hope *you* don't."

Toward the end of my sophomore year, I cut my hair short, and drank beer every night in Village bars. Mother stopped asking where I went. She picked on me for wearing fly-front jeans. It's the style, I told her, and she pretended to believe me. Her mother was dying, and Sam was horribly depressed. But most troubling, Jan, who'd just divorced Danny, was seeing him again. "He loves me," she cried.

"Luv," mimicked Mother, twisting her mouth in scorn.

One night a young woman marched up to me at a Greenwich Village bar. "I'm a philosopher from Brooklyn College," she said. "Who are you?"

"An actress, a student."

"You look unhappy."

"I am."

A sophomore—a dead ringer for the old film comedian Jack Oakie—Sally found me "boring, but necessary." I had no interest whatever in dating young men.

"We think you're afraid," said Dr. Adelson. The royal "we."

But I didn't feel afraid. Did he hope to force my feelings from their hiding places merely by naming them?

"I'm not afraid."

"How do you know?" I was silent. "There's something called the unconscious," he began pompously. I've heard of it, I wanted to snap, but let him go on, silent under siege: "Did you ever consider that you're not homosexual at all? That your heterosexual feelings are in fact very strong?" Now, how the hell did he know that? "You need help," he concluded.

"That may be, but I don't think I'm getting it here." My belligerence startled me.

"Why not?"

"Coming here makes me feel worse."

"That's part of the process."

"Is it? A wound hurts worst when it's healing? How bad is it supposed to get?"

"We don't understand you," he conceded.

"*What* don't you understand?" I demanded. It wasn't the first time I'd heard this. Mrs. Provet had told me at school, "I look at other students and can tell their backgrounds at a glance. You! I don't know you. I can't find you. I don't know where you're coming from." It hurt me deeply.

"All you have to do is come here," persisted Dr. Adelson.

I had the habit of picking my cuticles until they bled; one was bleeding then. "See?" he said, glancing at my hand.

"So what?"

"Doesn't that take energy from your acting?"

He wasn't wrong; the tone of his voice was wrong. There was no kernel of warmth between us. Nothing in his eyes urged me to speak. To whatever I said: "Why do you feel that way?" he'd ask glumly. Were all my perceptions symptoms? Something else troubled me: he wanted to know how I felt about him; it was impossible to tell him. I couldn't bear to hurt his feelings and didn't know why. Insane child! If the foundation of art is truth, couldn't I see lies weaken it? Didn't I realize the extent of my rage? Were the roots so fraught with pain, I couldn't feel them strangling?

One day I heard from the waiting room a furious outburst from Dr. Adelson's previous appointment, a young boy of ten or eleven. "Why don't you leave me alone? Why do I have to come here? I'm just like everyone else!" The youngster ran out. A moment later I was amazed to see Dr. Adelson emerge, face lit in a huge, Cheshire grin. Peering into a colleague's open door, he mumbled, "Things are beginning to boil."

"Great! How?"

"I got him to the point . . ." He shut the door; I heard no more. But I knew with a certainty I couldn't explain that his satisfaction had less to do with the child's welfare than his own pride in having tortured out his rage. "I got him to the point"? He wouldn't speak that way about me.

His poker face couldn't hide his disapproval of Sally. It provoked my spite. I'd never admit she repelled me physically. She'd been urging me lately to quit therapy "because they think what we feel is sick." Today I was ready to do so. Ten minutes into our session, I told Dr. Adelson I wouldn't be back.

"Again?" He looked mildly annoyed. "They always come back."

"Do they?" I felt keenly his impudence and disrespect. Not I, I thought, not now. When I'd made it known I was serious:

"You know, of course, we'll have to tell your mother about Sally," he warned. "It's the law."

"Why didn't you observe it last week?" I gibed.

"Why are you so angry?" he returned, with a pleasant smile. I

51

knew he'd rub my nose in it, the way Barbara rubbed my nose in my feces—a memory I'd been too inhibited to confess.

After her meeting with Dr. Adelson, Mother approached me stiffly. "He told me to be sympathetic," she began. I was ready to laugh out loud. But because she was troubled, I reminded her of her old bedtime confession to me: as "a young girl on fire" she'd asked certain friends "to do bad with her."

"You didn't tell *him* that, did you?"

"No! It's just . . . with Sally it's no worse than that."

Dr. Adelson tried to get me to return through the intervention of a social worker. But I was adamant. "I think Carol has had enough," asserted Mother. "Now we'd like to file out like ladies." And like ladies we did.

Of how much self-sabotage was I aware? Much was unconscious; but more was conscious than I had courage to admit. I couldn't confess to Dr. Adelson the root causes of my spite: how long Barbara had kept me in darkness; how hard Jan had kicked me in the stomach for refusing to be her slave. Because it seemed that, given the opportunity, he would do the very same things.

Shortly after I left him, I'd wake up sobbing from dreams of just being held by a woman. Is there a category for what I was? Homospiritual, not homosexual? What I knew, but could not admit, was that beneath my lesbian pose—the lie I thought made me interesting—was a desperate cry for notice. Somebody had to take care of me.

Chapter Five

*I*n the second term of my sophomore year, I received the grade of S-minus in acting. It was given to me by bald, sharp Mr. Olvin, who was the butt of so many student complaints that everyone cheered when he lost his job. How he wagged his ego at our expense! Still, the grade rankled. It meant he didn't like me. Dr. Adelson hadn't liked me. Who can like a bitter child who repudiates your every word? Fifteen-year-old tough kid, a cigarette dangling from my lips the day a classmate spat out at me, "Why do you have to be different?" I didn't know, I couldn't say. I knew only that high school had become a prison to me: the clanging of bells between classes, the interminable academic lectures I made no effort to understand.

One day in Dr. Dycke's class, I quit in the middle of an exercise. "I broke," I said, using actors' parlance for fractured concentration. But really I could have gone on. I think both of us knew that. She spoke to me afterward. "You have the power to thrill an audience." What was wrong? Could I tell her? I started to cry. "Cry," she urged, "cry. This is the first time I really see you. I *want* to see you. What is it? Tell me."

Something was whipping around, slicing me up inside. Because I lacked the courage to fail, I failed. But we learn by failing, she insisted. There is no other way but to be willing to fall on our faces, and in what better place than a classroom? How tell her I couldn't learn, that when God saw fit, He inspired me; but when despair wiped out my will, no technique could save me? My thoughts of God were secret, secret as a crime. Nor did I admit—how could I?—that instead of listening in class, I'd note the inflections of her voice and face each time she glanced my way and later added them up to see if they seemed to show love.

I suffered enormous guilt. Over what? I couldn't say. Most kids pretended to be something they were not. I pretended to be what I was. For example, if I felt shy, I'd sooner play up that shyness than make an effort to communicate. Yes, but what did the shyness mask? I didn't know.

She recommended God and psychotherapy, in that order. The latter was all the rage, with good reason. ("I'm all for it!") That I'd had a disappointing first experience shouldn't discourage my pursuing it. Had she ever wanted to act? I asked, eager to change the subject. Of course. But she lacked the talent. She was no fantast for whom the bubble must burst. Her strict Danish father forbade that possibility the day he gathered her and her sisters into the parlor and pointed to each in turn: "'Mary will sell, Alice will nurse, and Marjorie will teach.' And here I am!"

Marjorie Dycke! Every Monday afternoon at three o'clock I'd knock on her office door. I spent the week rehearsing my troubles. I wanted to confess something terrible, but didn't know what. That I loved her was out of the question. Instead, "I think I'm becoming a lesbian."

She said I wasn't; I said I was. I felt insulted! I so wanted to be. I'd lie awake nights recalling her voice, her eyes—large, gray, almond-shaped eyes. She still called me "my pet"; told me how to wear my hair (like hers, brushed back from the forehead in a bun), and to buy suits (pronounced "syutes"). She was nearly six feet tall and wore them well. My favorite was a wine-colored silk. At night I pretended she held me, that's all. Ours was a spiritual love that sex would only dirty.

Eventually I confessed about Sally, and my nightly treks to the Village. I wanted to stop; I couldn't. Something drew me there. I felt caught in hell. My home life was frightening. But if nothing mattered except acting, she asked, why didn't I behave accordingly? No, I didn't pretend to be what I was. She begged to differ: "You're guilty? Then just stop doing things that make you guilty."

"Like what?"

"Break it off with Sally. You don't love her, do you?"

I might have known, from the ease with which I did it, the price I'd pay in guilt. But go or stay, I'd have paid.

Several months earlier, Sally had introduced me to Claudia, a petite, black-eyed, intensely enthusiastic German-Jewish piano student of twenty-two. Claudia earned her keep ushering at New York City Center, where she got me a weekend job.

"How wonderful!" exclaimed Dr. Dycke. "You can see all the shows free."

Judy Holiday, whose comedic honesty Dr. Dycke had praised, was playing in Garson Kanin's *Born Yesterday*. With my salary, I bought her a ticket for the Saturday night performance, and, switching places with another usher, arranged to seat her myself. She wanted to repay me for the ticket. When I told her I got it for nothing, she raised an eyebrow at me. She enjoyed the show enormously. I heard her happy laugh throughout. "Wasn't it wonderful?" she asked me afterward over ice cream at Howard Johnson's.

"Yes," I agreed, unable to meet her eye. She was munching a maraschino cherry when she told me she had something special to ask me, but this was not the time.

"Oh, *what?*"

"I'm still thinking about it."

"Oh, please, tell me!" She drew back, repelled. I'd begged her—all right, I whined—but hadn't she urged me to express my true feelings? ("Be free. Open yourself!") I was just too giddy-glad. I bowed my head in shame and beat myself for it all night long.

That Monday in her office: "You've been through so much," she began. "If you could undo the damage, start again. . . . How would you feel about finding another home?"

"Another home? Whose?" I was astonished.

She looked at me a long moment. "Let me think about it. I'll need to make some inquiries."

I walked for hours afterward. What inquiries? Did she know a couple who might want me? Or did she herself? A fire shot through my veins. I hoped it as keenly as I dreaded it. Could it be she was afraid to admit it? Was she waiting for me to ask? I was frightened, too. A divorced woman of thirty-five, how would she manage it? She!—with whom I couldn't even eat ice cream. But I was never to know her mind. A few days later in her office:

"Really, at fifteen I think you're too old to change families," she said frankly. Wouldn't I reconsider psychotherapy? After all, Mount Sinai wasn't the only clinic in New York. She could, if I wished, put in a call to the Payne Whitney Outpatient Clinic at New York Hospital.

⌒

Dr. Frank Fitzpatrick was a young man, stoop-shouldered and unnaturally thin, with light, delicately boned hands and a receding hairline. After I ran down the events of my life for him, he asked why I had come.

"Something's stifling me. Did Dr. Dycke tell you?"

"*You* tell me. What do you want?"

"Liberation," I answered.

"Liberation," he mused. "That's a large order."

He explained that I needed to "work through" my experiences, not simply rattle them off. "Give me your feelings. I'm not here to be spared."

I began to relive the beatings, the incidents in the closet, and the movies. My feelings came back full force, and with them— miracle of miracles—my acting! I grew freer. After a successful exercise, before she'd ask for class comments, Dr. Dycke's quick glance of approval would set my nerves tingling. When she said, "That's excellent," I was in raptures for the week.

Dr. Fitzpatrick suggested that by getting at the root of my experiences, I might eventually move an audience to the extent I had been moved. From this I understood that the more I suffered for the doctor, the better I was doing. The subject of masturbation had come up. I'd just admitted my old habit of stopping before climax, when he was interrupted by a phone call.

"Where were we?" he asked, resuming his seat.

"We were disgusting masturbation."

It slipped out; by the jolt of his head I knew he'd heard it. When I found courage finally to look up, he said calmly, "You've just told me what you feel about it, though why you feel obliged . . ."

"To get it out of my system! Didn't you say I had to?"

But he wasn't the only doctor who'd ask for my feelings only to recoil from them.

It was Payne Whitney policy for therapists to interview the parents of their adolescent patients. He saw my mother only once. "She's a very sick and unhappy woman," he told me. I'd known it all along—not only by her cruelty, but in her rare, tender moments. Since her own mother's recent death, she'd been unable to swallow meat. "It'd be like eating Mama's flesh," she confided. Then shyly, "You're *me*, do you know that, Carol? You're my flesh and blood."

I continued to take refuge in fantasy. The Italian genius Eleonora Duse had written at the end of her acting career, "Some day another woman will come, young, beautiful, a being all of fire and flame, and will do what I have dreamed."* I was certain I was she. But Dr. Fitzpatrick had warned me to keep a check on fantasy. I must be active all the time.

My schoolwork progressed. Sense and emotion memory exercises led to animal improvisations, which sent us to the zoo. For relaxation exercises, our new teacher, the young director Sidney Lumet, had me take a shower like an eggbeater, then become a cross-eyed typewriter. The entire department adored him. I, of course, kept my crush a secret as I listened in the corridors to arguments, not about which of us he liked best, but who among us loved him more. This was the trap of our training: we could be more enamored of our feelings than the objects that inspired them.

Toward the end of our sophomore year, students who did poorly in acting were "counseled out." A whole day was set aside for individual conferences. "For those whose hearts will be broken," began Dr. Dycke, when an angry student challenged, "You think you people know enough to judge who should be kicked out?" Dr. Dycke cringed. "*Counseled* out." Then, "Yes, after two years we think we can judge. Better now than later," she added.

When my turn finally came, I peeked my head in the door to find Mr. Lumet and Dr. Dycke conferring. Both looked up at once.

"We love you," assured Mr. Lumet.

At our last weekly assembly that year Dr. Dycke announced, "We have two potentially great actresses in our midst: Sandra and Carol. Sandra expresses her gifts now, but Carol cannot."

---

*Eleonora Duse, *Actors on Acting* (New York: Crown, 1954), 414.

I was so jealous of Sandra, jealous of her freedom. Other students attacked her: "She uses people," they complained. "So what?" I countered. "She's a great actress—or will be." Brilliant as she was, Sandra hadn't yet shed her New York accent, whereas my diction had been standard from the start. Nevertheless, in the hallways and after school, I took on her speech and mannerisms, and by so doing, "became" her. It didn't alarm me—why should it?—that the harder my life seemed, the more easily I slipped into another's. A faultless ear for dialect, an easy ability to be wholly this way one day, wholly that way the next; I could become what I admired as well as what I loathed.

I was sixteen when I first wondered what social characteristics distinguish the so-called multiple-personality psychotic from a genius like Shakespeare, who contained within him many men, and many women, too. What, besides self-control? I'd imagine him relaxing in a tavern after a performance. He'd be the only one no one would remember. He'd be too busy watching us—not in the bug-eyed way that announces how well he observed. Oh, no! He'd fade right into the shadows, the better to catch us unaware.

But my immediate problem was Sandra, whom Dr. Fitzpatrick advised me to befriend. An attractive teenager, she was fashionably slim, excellent in academics, intelligent, and calm. She bore no trace of suffering—but to achieve those results? She'd learned to channel it! I must do the same. Who were her friends? Kids who did only adequately in acting but were her equals or better in academics. Though she wouldn't be my friend (I *did* try), whenever either of us played, we'd look to the other for that silent nod of approval: that was good. She was also astonishingly mature. She wanted a home and family and questioned whether an acting career might conflict with her personal needs.

"Do you think I'll ever be normal like Sandra?" I asked Dr. Fitzpatrick one day.

"You'll never be normal," he explained, "because of certain experiences. The point is to get as close to it as possible."

I believed I was on my way the morning Dr. Dycke called me into her office. Something was wrong. Another teacher who'd witnessed the spontaneous embrace of two students in the hallway overheard the passing comment of a third: "Girls! Don't be like Carol Hebald." Dr. Dycke warned me in no uncertain terms to keep my mouth shut. Her words drew blood. I believe they were as difficult for her to say as for me to hear. She was sorry no one had taught me how to be, but it was time I learned. I was inappropriate. My behavior was inappropriate. But my thoughts and feelings were not. Never mind! Shut them, hide them, erase them! I felt, for the first time, the wretched awareness that she didn't care. She looked at me, and for an instant I saw the implacable gaze of her father. She wasn't openly angry; that was not her way. But her coldness was withering. I felt it like a knife. She went on to criticize my choice of friends. "What do you have in common with Gloria and Nina? Look at Sandra, look at Suzanne. Who are *their* friends?" Perky Suzanne, I thought nastily, she'll do well. She sucks up very nicely to all the right people. Aloud I said, "What's the matter with Nina and Gloria? They're perfectly nice girls."

"They're on their way out."

Dr. Dycke should not have said that to me. Nevertheless, before the start of my junior year, I discarded my fly-front jeans, dressed in simple skirts and blouses, and let my hair grow. I, too, had had a father. It was he who'd given me strength. He, Mrs. Kessler, Joseph Geiger, and, though I couldn't admit it then, Dr. Dycke, too. I owed it to them to succeed. Further than this I dared not think: What I renounced was determined by what I was anxious to keep.

～

Sally's friend Claudia, the piano student and City Center usher, had introduced me to her teacher, the distinguished German pianist Kurt Appelbaum, who invited me to a musical gathering of his students. There he asked Claudia to play Beethoven's *Waldstein* for us. She began, stopped midway, then rose.

"I can't play it."

"Stay put," commanded Appelbaum, who joined her at the piano and, playing the passage that had stumped her, illustrated it in words: "Listen! A flock of geese is soaring. . . . A small bird sings from the mountain. . . . Now he's calling wildly. . . . Play." He rose and she began. Her notes were chopped and strained. What was the problem? He discussed it first with her, then with the group, when abruptly, "I think we've had enough of Claudia," he said. She returned to her seat. A young man was called to the piano.

The blood drained from her face; she sat motionless in despair. Why couldn't I confess that her difficulty was similar to mine? Sharing it might have freed us both. But I wouldn't admit failure. I knew only that I had to dissociate myself from it—and her. She frightened me. Her temper was huge. She'd rage at me over a thousand imagined slights. She gave of herself completely. Why didn't I?

Two years before, as a student at Black Mountain College, where her mother still taught piano, she'd been hospitalized for a mental breakdown. After her release, she left school to study with Appelbaum, when news came of her beloved father's death. Appelbaum took care of her for weeks. Claudia adored her mother. Poor child! Everyone knew Mrs. Erlbach was ashamed of her daughter. And no one but Appelbaum cared. In fact, except for him, the group of German Jews she introduced me to, escapees from Hitler's Germany, all laughed at Claudia's intensity. Jewish intensity, was it?

Among them was Aliberti, whom Appelbaum recommended to me.

"I'm not a singer," I had explained. "But as an actress, I need to develop my voice."

"Naturally. I have a neighbor upstairs, a superb conductor, a fine teacher."

Chapter Six

*C*laudia is very peculiar," announced elegant, stately Aliberti, the middle-aged Austrian opera conductor, whose real name was Herbert Herzfeld.
"Peculiar, how?"

"Overintense about all the wrong things," quipped his lover,
Tommy, on his way out the door. An obviously gay young actor
with a deep, Mississippi drawl, Tommy tipped his cap at a rakish
angle and bade us adieu. A few minutes later, in the middle of a
singing exercise, I felt dizzy and started to weave. "A too-deep intake of breath?" guessed Aliberti, when all went black before me.
I held tightly to the piano for support. He let me rest a moment,
then, striking the exercise chord, "Again?"

"Nyam, nyam, nyam, nyam, nyam, nyam, nyam," I intoned,
and nearly fainted. He led me to a chair. Was I all right?

"Not quite." I shut my eyes, then sighed out at seeming random what I'd been waiting anxiously to confess: "I wish I didn't
have to see a psychiatrist."

"Oh, are you going?" he asked, grinning hugely. But I still
looked a bit green. Would I like some coffee? Oh, yes!

"May one ask why?" he called out from the kitchen. "Wait, I'll
be right there."

I told him about Dr. Dycke. "Dr. *Who?*" he inquired, because
dyke is slang for *butch*. I smiled. "Tell me all about her," he invited warmly, and draping his leg over the arm of his chair, sipped
his coffee and listened. Was I in therapy just for *that?* Yes! It was
interfering with my work.

"It is an illness, isn't it?"

"It's a maladjustment," he explained simply. But he'd known others who'd tried the "inexact science" of psychiatry with extremely limited results. "And for people like us I think it's. . . . Well, I don't think you need it."

People like us. Was he also? Of course, and always had been. Could I have fallen in love with him otherwise?

It happened after one of my Nyam-nyam warm-ups: "You have a tremendous range," he said, "disregarding the tone." I laughed out loud. His wit and charm were immense. I loved his Austrian accent. My father had had one, too. They even bore the same initials: Henry Hebald/Herbert Herzfeld. But what made him change his name? Claudia "had it" from Appelbaum that he'd been caught, in violation of union rules, conducting a nonunion orchestra under the alias Armando Aliberti. The union, thinking him too good a musician to oust, punished him by making him keep the alias. A strange, though not impossible, story that struck a fraudulent key in my mind.

Allergic to popular culture ("your simply ghahstly mush"), Aliberti was obliged to train my poor voice on show tunes so that in time I might audition for musicals. One day, having sailed wholeheartedly into the lyrics of "Hello Young Lovers, Wherever You Are," I, enlightened by experience, cautioned my young friends "to be truuue" because "I've been in love like youuuh." Reading my fantasy, Aliberti, at the keys, gazed up at me with a smile of utmost tenderness. I smiled back broadly—too broadly—and had to stop. Brows raised in bewilderment, he struck the passage chord loudly. Was something wrong? Embarrassed, I began again. Again he smiled, and again I grinned and met his mock-stern look. Finally, when I had ended, "You are *very* cute," he said.

I feasted for weeks on the memory.

He'd teased me as one would tease a child in a bit of harmless fun. But through it I saw he adored me. There was no doubt he adored me. Oh, the eye deceives the mind with such dexterity! Entrenched in fantasy, I'd shut the door of my room and curl up in bed. Yesterday I'd glimpsed a brown silk smoking jacket hanging on his bathroom door. Was it his or Tommy's? His! Now my head was on that jacket and he was stroking my hair. We spoke of this and that, posing and supposing problems, reliving yesterday's lesson, preplaying the content of tomorrow's. In solitude I was never alone. I moved, his camera clicked, his mind perceived my inmost thoughts. If only others would let me be!

At the mere prospect of meeting Claudia, I'd grow suddenly exhausted. But I was not one to cancel a date, not at the last moment, and never with Claudia, who needed me more and more. She had Appelbaum, I had Aliberti. Like two children comparing fathers, she thought hers superior to mine: "Appelbaum says Aliberti's a stuffed shirt and a snob."

"Who the hell is Mr. Appelbaum?"

Aliberti a stuffed shirt? The son of a Catholic obstetrician, he spoke highly of Vienna University, where his father had trained.

"You were raised a Catholic?"

"Yes," he answered, and quickly changed the subject.

Herzfeld a Catholic? Had his family converted? If so, when? Another fraudulent note? Perhaps I wasn't the only liar. Not to put a nasty cast on it, it does take one to know one. But did the Nazi regime, which would have killed him in any case as a homosexual, in subtle ways rub off? He hated his mother almost as much as I hated mine. Or did I admit hating mine because he hated his? I don't know! We agreed passionately on everything we hated:

"I wish all children were born at the age of nine," he declared.

"So do I."

"I hate people who get uncontrollably drunk."

"So do I."

"I hate people who have outbursts."

"So do I!"

I hate people. . . . I hate people. Oh, so did I!

"I hate words," I exclaimed one day.

"Then, my dear girl, I suggest you become a mime."

No, seriously, certain words made my flesh crawl: "*Intention,* for example. At school they're always asking, 'What's your character's intention,' implying she always knows it beforehand. Stanislavsky called it objective—conscious, unconscious, and preconscious," I added, drawing deeply on my cigarette.

"More coffee?"

"A smidgen, thanks."

Pouring me a brimful, "What's a conscious objective?" he asked.

"A true one? Under emotional stress: to fight for control."

"And a false one?"

"To show one's struggle. It leads to inorganic actions. Instead of restraining tears, one tries to force them out. *We* don't work that way."

"Don't we?"

Aliberti disapproved heartily of Stanislavsky. The actors he admired dazzled with their brilliance. They didn't feel, they thought and planned meticulously each and every effect.

"But to think without feelings?"

"They think with them. They act without them."

"But it's ridiculous to assume—even brilliantly—the outer shell of a character and expect to be believed. Every actress worth her salt knows that knit-browed pose of listening to indicate listening because one isn't listening at all!" Oh, that I knew in life what I knew in acting!

"Ah, but if one is a craftsman—!" he argued.

"Look," I interrupted, "if I leave a concert praising the violinist's craft, it couldn't have been very good. I was supposed to have heard the music! The actors you admire draw attention to themselves at the expense of the play!"

"I'm still not convinced," he said uncertainly.

I was excited. It meant he wanted to discuss it further—with *me*.

I don't know why my feelings for Aliberti, which differed only in degree from those I'd had for Dr. Dycke, coincided with my sudden, overwhelming hatred for her. Of course she sensed it. I had long since stopped our Monday afternoon talks when she cornered me one morning in the hallway and asked coyly, somewhat nastily, "What's the matter? Don't you love me anymore?" I said nothing. She walked away.

Aliberti's opera students came early in the day. During my thrice-weekly after school lessons, when Tommy was out making acting rounds, occasionally the telephone rang. At Aliberti's "*Wie geht*s?" I'd wander over to his bookshelves and make mental note of his titles. Later I'd find them in the library and read them through his eyes. Our hours together passed in heated discussions over coffee on the ideal life of the artist: what Goethe wrote to Schiller—"Whatever genius does *as* genius is done unconsciously"—and how Schiller worked, with a rotten apple core under his nose to shut out all other distractions.

"When you were my age, did you feel about music as I do about acting?" I asked.

Not quite, but he understood it, and suggested wisely that I approach it from the vantage point of an artisan, rather than an artist. "It's a job, an important one, not a religion."

"What else do I have?" No answer. "What else is there *to* me?" I pressed.

But instead of taking the bait, he picked on my appearance: "If your mother can afford to give you singing lessons, she can afford to buy you clothes."

"I don't like her taste."

"Insist on her buying what you like."

I remember the two-piece dress with pleated skirt and woolen jacket I wore to our lesson that Sunday:

"You look stunning," he exclaimed with satisfaction.

"*Ja?* I have a party later."

I tossed the lie off casually. He mustn't think I had nowhere to go. To be out alone was a mark of shame. I had a terror he'd spot me somewhere and think, "Poor thing. Doesn't she have any friends?"

One day at lesson's end, I complained that our relationship was unequal: "I tell you everything about me, and you confide nothing. Don't you have any problems? Inner or outer?" I added.

He was pleased; I saw it. "Well, life is expensive," he admitted. "Not food, of course, but rent . . ."

I raved about him at school and got him several students.

"I should start paying you a commission," he joked.

"Oh, no!" I protested. Then, "You know I'm graduating from high school in a few months. I wonder . . . could you be my acting teacher?"

"You mean next fall?"

"I mean right now."

He paused. "I'm not sure I'd be right."

"Yes, you would." He thought again, and agreed to try it.

Now, in return for my usher's salary, I'd be seeing him four times a week. I had shut out all other relationships—what did I need them for?—when Claudia sent me a luncheon invitation to her Greenwich Village railroad flat. We'd been excellent friends; I owed her at the very least the courtesy of an explanation for my silence.

"I've been preoccupied with school and lessons," I began. "And you know my sister's getting married again."

Yes, she understood that. Still, she assumed I cared.

"No, don't. What I'm trying to say . . . I don't think I have the capacity."

"The capacity?" Suddenly she was shouting, "I am a human being, too! Do you understand that?"

"Yes," I said quietly.

"No, I don't think you do!" Had I nothing more to say? No? "Then leave," she howled. "Immediately!" I rushed in terror out the door.

Early for my lesson next day, I was watching the lobby clock when Appelbaum approached me from the elevator. After an awkward exchange of greetings, I thanked him again for recommending Aliberti. Then, "How's Claudia?" I asked.

"Ach! Cloudia's under a cloud," he quipped sadly. "She misses you."

I shook my head, "What shall I do?"

"You have a lesson now? Ring my bell after, and we'll talk."

Awaiting me in his foyer, she rushed up to embrace me when Appelbaum checked her sharply, "Claudia's just leaving."

"I am," she said solemnly, and grabbing her coat, held her eyes on me until she shut the door.

Yes, she'd put him up to this. "She's afraid she's lost you for good."

"She has. I don't, I can't care! I don't know why she's so insistent."

"She's a little bit in love with you, no?" I bowed my head in acknowledgment. "You will fall in love one day," he said, "with a man or woman, I don't know. I hope it will be a man." In the meantime, I must keep my distance from Claudia. "Don't let her embrace you. If you meet her on the street, greet her warmly, then excuse yourself. 'Sorry, I'm in great hurry'" he demonstrated.

Kurt Appelbaum was that rare combination of consummate artist and first-rate human being. Claudia had insisted that the first always implies the second. Romantic child! If only it did.

Upstairs, Aliberti and I had read from *Faust,* my Gretchen to his Heinrich. It went well; how should it not?

~

I didn't attend my high school graduation. Nor was I given a role in the senior production of Jean Giraudoux's *The Madwoman of Chaillot.* Sandra won the Drama Award. Dr. Dycke's punishment for my fickleness was complete. Though I often dreamed of her, I never saw or spoke with her again.

Just before summer my sister married her second husband, Bob, who had been drafted into the army and would soon go off to Korea. A history major at NYU, Jan continued to live at home.

And I parted company with Dr. Fitzpatrick, who believed we'd reached a point of diminishing returns. I'd probably need therapy at a later date. In the meantime, he urged me again to keep active. I'd be subject to pitfalls of mood, along with thousands of other people. It was all a question of degree. I was welcome to keep in touch—that is, to phone him with specific problems. Was I pleased, he asked finally, that having come to him with homosexual needs, I now had heterosexual ones? Of course.

As Claudia was my only woman friend (Merna had married

and moved away), he was by no means pleased I'd stopped seeing her. I'd been in treatment long enough to know I needed the reality contact. "There was value in your friendship with Claudia," he said. And there was.

How did I feel in her presence and in the presence of so many others I'd see by doctor's prescription? Even as they spoke I missed myself!—my books, music, fantasies, comfort in dreams. What I didn't realize was that if I couldn't listen to others, neither could I listen to myself.

All right! Having spent the greater part of my life in an unconscious fantasy of heaven, I could not, without an immense effort of will, follow the most rudimentary conversation or read a newspaper. I had reason to escape, that's established. But what about other people?

When I read Rilke's dictum, "Works of art are of an infinite loneliness,"* I thought solitude prerequisite to it. What errors in judgment we make when we choose to become ill. Does it not seem I chose it, not consciously of course, but by stealth? Was I stupid from too much pain—too stupid to realize that the actor, like every artist, draws sustenance from life? How deny myself human relationships and expect to come alive onstage? Yet the words are scrawled in my diary: "For me, nourishment in yearning—only and always. I want to want, not to have."

How should I have known that wanting itself can fade? That my pitfalls of mood occurred in direct response to the prison I was creating?

---

*In *Letters to a Young Poet*, trans. M. D. Herter Norton (New York: Norton), 29.

Chapter Seven

*V*ery early this morning I fell asleep at my desk. In a dark, airless dream I heard a gentle woman say, "Oh, my dear child." When a dangling string hit my forehead I knew I was again in the closet. I moved my head and hands, caught the string, and pulled it, and a bare bulb gave light. The closet became a room, a pleasant little square room with two intricately carved wooden doors. Behind one was a down-spiraling staircase, behind the other, one spiraling up. Were the interior stairwells connected? I don't know. Nor did I bother to look for an exit, because in my little room I felt happy.

I awoke freshly reminded that I'm in a study I may leave whenever I choose, and though I stay to reenter the past, I need not lose my balance doing so. Yet I've been dillydallying for weeks now because I still can't answer why I strayed so far from my nature. I've hit a snag; my thoughts are tangling. There's no way out but back: the long descent into terror, the frequent flights of fantasy, failures that broke promise to my hopes. For on the eve of my eighteenth year, I neither saw nor cared to see the torment that drove me or why, once I had fallen, I couldn't pick myself up.

~

My apprenticeship at the Marblehead Summer Theater in 1952 began a week before my high school graduation, which I was immensely relieved to miss. But I was slow and got on badly with the others. Oh, I could sweep and scour toilets well enough. But when it came to setting lights or scenes, I was told repeatedly to get out of the way. I'd thumb through piles of old costumes, or take buses to nearby Salem, where I'd gorge on Chinese food. That summer, I gained twenty pounds. I wasn't even asked to audition for the one half-decent apprentice role. Why ask *why* when I knew: my high school failures were repeating themselves. My past not only bore upon my present, it was already predicting my future. I missed Aliberti dreadfully and wrote him a desperate letter, to which he sensibly replied, "Please remember you are an apprentice not in order that the American Theater may learn about you, but that you might learn about it." He was planning a brief holiday in the area and would try to stop by for a visit. But he never came.

My disappointment was offset by the arrival of a traveling performance of Molnár's comic masterpiece *The Play's the Thing,* with Luther Adler and Herbert Berghof. The female lead was played by Herbert's wife, Uta Hagen, whose work I'd worshipped for years. Assigned to be her personal apprentice, I was ironing her costume for the opening, when a short, middle-aged roué with quick, blue, berry-ripe eyes peered out at me from his dressing room. "Are you local talent?" he asked.

"Oh, no! I'm an actress from New York."

"I'm Luther Adler." He took a little bow. Then, "If I had a daughter who wanted to be an actress, I'd beat her with a broomstick."

"Oh? Why is that?"

"Have supper with us after the show and I'll tell you," he offered warmly, and pirouetted back on his heel.

I joined them every night for boilermakers and hard-boiled eggs. Everyone was on a diet! Afterward, Luther took me to the woods for sex. So began my third affair, which would span the

next several years, and with them a change of heart perceptible
to me in retrospect as something frighteningly sudden. My vow
of discipline by hunger gave way to pride in the sexual appetite
I'd known as a very young child. Should I not be proud? I wondered. Why then did God endow me with it? My faith in Him, dependent on the luck He tossed my way, was broken. It seemed
He'd broken faith with *me*.

One night, at season's end, I met a policeman at a local fair
who found me attractive enough to seduce. From this quick, care-
less encounter—in which neither of us had used protection—I
returned to New York feeling dirty and misused. I'd begun making acting rounds and working nights as a telephone solicitor for
mutual funds, when I discovered I was pregnant. I told Mother,
who, ever efficient in emergencies, phoned Dr. Fitzpatrick for
the name of an abortionist. A Catholic with a New York State license to protect, he rightly refused. Why couldn't I give birth?
Mother wouldn't hear of it. The day he warned her that an abortion might make me "emotionally upset," she took me on the
subway to our family doctor, who, in response to my predica-
ment, groaned, "Oh, no!" He handed her the number of an ac-
quaintance, who would come with an assistant to our home. To
me he snarled, "Get the hell out of here. I don't want to look at
you."

The following week two men came to the house. With the door
shut and the shades drawn, one held me down while the other
performed the abortion without an anaesthetic.

After my recovery, despite Mother's pleas to stay, I moved
across town to a furnished room near Aliberti. I resumed my
evening job and, to better earn my keep, studied shorthand and
typing at the Speedwriting Institute. I mastered shorthand, but
repeatedly flunked typing. The teacher made merciless fun of

me: "The lowest test score belongs, as usual, to Carol." The day she asked me in class, "Do you have a problem with coordination, dear, or are you just a klutz?" I walked out, never to return.

◇

Dr. Fitzpatrick had had reason to fear my upset. Although abortion is no sin in my family, I felt it keenly. Late one night Claudia called, and finding me barely able to speak, hung up to alert Aliberti, who phoned ten minutes later. Would I like to come over? Tommy was out of town.

We talked for hours. Claudia had "heard suicide" in my voice. Why? I couldn't tell him. A good friend, he gave me pajamas and toothbrush, and made me stay the night. I crept into his bed. "Are you going to sleep now?" he asked guardedly. "Yes." Then he kissed me on the cheek, and turned away. I lay at his side all night listening to him breathe.

In the morning: "Next time you decide to commit suicide," he said, "please do so at a reasonable hour."

Justified or not, it cut me to the core. Nor did I consider his feelings in my letter that day when I declared that because I loved him, I was saying goodbye: "Thank you for my liberty," I signed off dramatically, and waited by the phone.

It rang the following afternoon. "Come on over," he said.

"I'd rather not."

"Come on over," he commanded.

Once there, I asked for my letter back.

"Why?" He smiled hugely.

"I don't want Tommy to find it." Whereupon Tommy emerged from the bedroom with a deep bow.

"Where are you off to, dear?" asked Aliberti.

"The movies." And he left.

"You showed it to him!"

In it I had confessed to the terrors and agonies he'd caused me by his relentless teasing.

"What teasing?"

"You don't remember that day I sang and you smiled and . . ."

"No."

"Did you know I loved you?" I asked him.

"Of course." Again the smile!

"How?"

"You can tell," he almost whined.

I started quickly for the door. He cried out, "Stay!" and made me sit down. "What is it you want?" he asked.

"More time with you."

"How much time do you think a person has?"

I got up again. "Sit down! Tell me."

"I can't."

"Confess."

I admitted I wanted to live with him—not sexually, never that. Did he know I waited for him at home every night? That he watched me wherever I went? Did he think that was something to laugh at? Finally, "You know I'm no singer. And I can't afford the acting lessons."

"Okay, we stop them!" Then, "Look. I don't want to lose you because . . . well, there are some people who simply make one feel *so* brilliant."

I burst out laughing; I couldn't help it.

What about Tommy? he asked. I admitted I loved him, too. "You love Tommy, too?" Then he held out his arms and wrapped me in a fierce embrace.

Our singing lessons ended; we were friends, but only for a little while.

"Call me," he'd say at the end of an awkward visit.

"Why don't you call me?"

"Really, darling, it's so much easier the other way."

But I felt too ashamed. I imagined Tommy answering and calling out, "It's her again."

And so the relationship ended. For years I looked for him on the street. From time to time, I'd spot Tommy, only to avert my gaze.

~

In the fall of 1953, I auditioned for Uta Hagen's scene study class. No sooner had I entered the room, than she asked, "Haven't we met before?"

"In Marblehead," I whispered. After a brief preparation, I played for her Gretchen's "Incline, O Maiden" prayer from *Faust*. When I'd finished, Miss Hagen's eyes were filled with tears. That evening she phoned to say how deeply I had moved her.

On the first day of class she walked briskly in the door and announced, "With one exception, your auditions were appalling."

"They were what?" someone shot back.

And Uta spelled: "A-P-P-A-L-L-I-N-G."

Afterward, her husband, Herbert Berghof, greeted me at the coatracks: "I heard about your Gretchen."

"It was okay," I answered limply, because the instant I saw him, I was overcome with shame at my fantasy that Luther had discussed me with him in Marblehead. ("How *was* she?" "Absolutely marvelous.")

For my first scene, I acted the Prussian orphan Manuela in Christa Winsloe's *Mädchen in Uniform*. It had gone beautifully in rehearsal, but in front of Uta, I froze. She strode up to me afterward: "What went wrong with the scene?" She waited; I couldn't speak. Her impatience frightened me. "You *pushed*," she exclaimed finally. I knew, but said nothing.

The following week, in a misguided effort to relax, I tried

mumbling my way through an easier role. After praising my partner, Uta turned to me: "Carol, I don't know what the hell you
were doing," she bristled. Had I bothered to read the play? Or
considered the reason for my presence on stage?

"Oh, it wasn't that bad," I muttered.

"Oh, yes it was!"

The class gasped. I sat down. The next scene was called to the
floor.

Afterward I walked to the Port Authority Bus Terminal and
bought a one-way ticket to Boston. Why Boston? I don't know. It
was a place to disappear. From the waiting area, I called Dr. Fitzpatrick, who by now was dividing his time between Payne Whitney and his private office, where I reached him.

"Don't go," he said. "Promise to come here first." I tore up the
ticket and walked uptown.

He sat, pale and thin, behind a quaint, old mahogany desk dec-
orated with several odd, precious antiques. On his side table lay
a rare edition of the Bible. At the end of the hour, I agreed to resume therapy with him at the clinic.

Several weeks passed before I acted again for Uta: this time a
cruel, love-starved schoolgirl who challenges her sentimental social worker with the retort, "Do you want to be my friend, Miss
Moffit?" at which tears sprang to my eyes. Uta leaned forward in
rapt attention. Fine teacher that she is, she asked immediately
how I'd prepared the scene so I might approximate its results in
the event of a long run. I told the truth: "According to the way
that play is written, this girl is right!"

Uta howled, "That's why it was so good!"

◇

In his final days, because Sam longed again for the trees and grass
of his youth, Mother moved to countrified Riverdale. Jan and

78

Bob set up housekeeping just across the way. I, in the meantime, was touring the East Coast as Pandora in a children's theater road company. Our last stop was the Brooklyn Academy of Music, from where, between shows, I made a surprise visit home.

Janice answered the door: "Sam just died," she said. "You'll have to cancel your tour."

I opened my mouth to speak. Instead, the shock caused my face to break out in an ear-to-ear grin that for several minutes I couldn't control. Mother sat quietly with Jan and Bob as Sam's covered body was removed. After the final performance, I moved back home, where my stepfather's name was never mentioned. It was as though he had never existed.

The happy event that year was my invitation into Uta's Friday professional class; I was her youngest student. "And one of my funniest," she'd said affectionately. Oh, how I adored her! That class was a little patch of heaven on earth. After pounding the pavements all week, we'd check our egos at the gate and play—not only the great characters of Shakespeare, Chekhov, and Strindberg, but those cut to type by lazy playwrights, whose essential work we did! We judged nothing. We assumed nothing. On the contrary: asked by our lazy playwright to act his "thoroughly despicable woman," we'd find twelve things about her that were good—to reverse her manufacturer's label, find out if she would wash. We had to embody her, discover the configurations of her spine. We'd map her out with objectives, obstacles, actions: what does she want, what's in her way, and how does she handle the stumbling blocks? We'd slip through the back door of her mind and ask humbly for something to share. She took us into her confidence. We brought her close, befriended her. And on that day *she* became *I*—oh, it was so exciting!—how am I "despicable?" we'd ask. Who in her own mind is despicable? Only someone good!

So I made rounds, and rehearsed scenes for class. And my affair with Luther continued. It was only my third, but he didn't believe it. Good girls didn't enjoy themselves so much, was that it?

"Why are you so quiet?" he asked one day. Thoughts criss-crossed in my mind. I kept forgetting what I wanted to say. I admired his work and had wanted to learn from him. But Luther was a target of the brutal McCarthy investigations, of which I knew nothing. I never read the paper and blush to admit I thought guerrilla warfare was fought by apes. So when I raised the subject of our work, he'd shut me up with, "The theater bores the shit out of me."

Discussions about men using women as sex objects were as prevalent in the early fifties as they are today. And because I never complained, Luther had fun sounding me out on the topic: he had a friend whose girl accused him of using her. "Maybe *she's* using *him*," he prompted. What did I think?

I tried to marshal my thoughts, let them assemble and take shape in my mind. Finally, when I answered, "How should I know?" Luther told me a joke: "Two goldfish were swimming around the bowl. One turned to the other and asked, 'Is today Thursday?'" Then, "I could only tell that to someone like you."

Someone as dumb? I didn't ask. But in fact I was using him, or wanted to. This came out inadvertently many years later, when, as a university professor on holiday, I audited Uta's class. Later we discussed my student days at college after I'd left acting, in particular what I'd learned from my professors.

"Did you sleep with them, too?" Uta asked me bluntly.

"No!" But her question shocked the truth out of me: "Not unless there was something to learn—and no other way to learn it."

Now it was her turn to gasp.

∽

In our Riverdale building complex lived a physics major at Columbia, a sensitive young man named Elliot who fell in love with me, but to whom I couldn't respond. Involved with an older, separated actor named Norman, I admitted to Mother my aversion to Elliot's touch. "Thinks no one's good enough for her," she muttered under her breath. "Gotta get knocked around a little bit." Each time Elliot brought me home, she complained, "I heard *him* talking all evening. *You* didn't open your mouth." I tried to defend myself. "I, I, I, I, I, I, I," she taunted; "me, me, me, me, me, me, me. . . . . There's murder in your eyes." Yes, because she put it there! And I let her—let her visit her wretchedness on me because she knew no other way to bear it. Is that why I stayed? Or was it the homely comforts, the familiarities, the crazy fits of laughter in the midst of our most furious fights, when one of us said something so absurd that a brief exchange of glances was all we needed to send the other into a hopelessly contagious jag?

When finally I broke with Elliot, "You don't count your blessings," he accused. "Why don't you take care of your mother?" I hated her as never before. But if I stayed because I needed a mother—any mother—she needed one more. How often had she reminded me she'd never been a child? Circumstances had insulted her enough. Her life was harder than mine. Twice widowed, she'd never lived alone. Women who did so were pathetic. Let Norman "use me" for sex; there was no danger he'd marry and take me away. Yet she insisted she wanted me married.

The days I went downtown to make rounds, I looked for Norman instead in coffee shops, agents' offices, and on the street. Was my life really so bleak? No. It was fun sometimes—so much fun—goofing off at the library, where I read Sartre's line "Hell is other people,"* the same day Dr. Fitzpatrick urged me "to relate." I knew *that* kind of confusion was essential. A named confusion was a joy to contemplate! It was the other kind that plagued me.

With Sam dead, Mother moved us back to Manhattan, to an apartment on West Seventy-sixth Street. I landed the role of Edelgard in Equity Library Theater's production of *Mädchen in Uniform*. Being in the all-female cast that also featured my classmates Barbara Barrie and Anne Meara was the happiest group experience I remember. I was part of something at last. The show was wonderful. Our director, the gifted Walt Witcover, managed not only to lead us beautifully into the play, but also to keep us in tow. Imagine! Thirty-one actresses and not one fight.

In accordance with union policy, we played our allotted week. Now, with reviews in hand and a list of agents who'd seen the show, I made rounds with newfound confidence: "Hi! Remember me?"

One morning the phone rang. The producer of the television program *Frontiers of Faith* had seen me in *Mädchen*. Was I available to play a young mother on Sunday's show? This was NBC—live TV before a national audience! I was overjoyed. Mother, returning from the grocer, had heard the tail end of our conversation.

"I got a job," I shrieked, "from *Mädchen!*"

"You weren't *that* good," she said.

She wouldn't comment on the NBC show. I didn't even ask if she'd watched. But audience response was good. Three weeks later, I was asked to play again.

---

*In his one-act play *No Exit*, trans. Stuart Gilbert (New York: Knopf, 1946), scene 5.

Home with Mother, I had only to cross the room for her to waddle like a baby in grotesque imitations of me. Not only was my success intolerable to her, my sister lockstepped at her side. A Phi Beta Kappa graduate of NYU, Jan had become a top-notch legal secretary. Who did I think I was, "living in the lap of luxury"? I should get a regular job, go to dances to meet men. Why couldn't acting be my hobby? She had no objection to that. They bit so viciously into me, always when things were going well, that I had to leave again.

I had moved to a furnished room and taken a job at Woolworth's, where one day Norman stepped up to the counter. Mother had phoned him that morning and begged him to intercede. He tried to "reason with me" for her sake. For this, I lost all respect for him and fell quickly and mercifully out of love. But pity for my mother brought me home.

Chapter Eight

I was still studying with Uta Hagen when, in 1955, she began rehearsals for the Broadway production of Ugo Betti's *Island of Goats*. The actress cast as Uta's daughter was failing badly. I was asked to audition for her role four times, the last, one week before the opening. After my third try, the director said he was thrown right out of his seat, "electrified" by what I did. Called a fourth time, I asked Uta what was going on. "I think you should read," was all she said. The failing actress, a washout compared to Uta, kept her role. But on opening night, I recognized my audition in her performance: verbal inflections, line readings, physical life. That this sort of betrayal and much worse happens in the theater every day didn't help me accept it. I could not throw off my hurt.

Crippled with sadness, I sought relief in lust. For this I was filled with guilt, except of course when I fell "in love" and thought with the heart of a child: give all, and you will receive. Sometimes I'd plead with a man to wait a little while before sex, to let me believe he cared. None would. Yet this mortification felt sweet; it kept me close to my father who, like me, found safety in numbers from the anguish of loneliness. He married my mother and became lonelier still. When she told him to go to a whore, he must have done just that. Toward the very end, I remember him standing in his pajamas under his arched bedroom door: "I am going to die," he told me. "Take me and put me somewhere close to you."

I want to skim quickly my final bout with promiscuity, and not from shame alone. The truth is, I don't remember my lovers half so well as my need of them. None exists in the light of any specific clarity, but rather, merge together in the darkness that gradually closed over me.

"You have a sad, wistful quality—very appealing," said Bob, a technician on *Frontiers of Faith,* who took me for coffee after my second appearance on the show. I remember a smiling bear of a man—furry, dark, forty (I wouldn't consider a man under forty). I looked modestly into my cup. Recently separated, Bob lived alone at the Bryant Hotel. Soon I had two lovers within a block of one another: Luther on Fifty-fifth Street and Bob on Fifty-fourth. In the grip of an obsession with Bob, I felt too frightened to speak normally with him on the phone. "You sound nervous," he'd say. "Something wrong?" I never told him he called too seldom, that when he did, I couldn't think of anything to say. I waited by the telephone and practiced my hello, wrote him letters I never mailed. One begins, "I'm writing because I want to talk to you, and I'm ashamed to call you up."

That year I was general understudy in F. Hugh Herbert's Broadway adaptation of *Marriage, Italian Style,* which he retitled *The Best House in Naples.* We opened on a Friday night at the Lyceum Theater and closed on Saturday. By the time I had made my debut at the matinée in place of ailing Renée Rogers, the original director, Claude Dauphin, had left the show. Two weeks later he asked me out:

"I love you," he declared at Le Pavillon. To which I managed a very meek "Thank you." No other man had ever said that to me! I showed him my first two poems. "Ah!" he cried, astonished. "But you are a great poet!"

"Oh, no," I said, "not that!"

"*Pardon!*" he murmured with a blush. He was leaving to direct a film in Saigon. Could I come with him? But I'd just gotten Equity permission to play Abigail in a nonunion performance of Arthur Miller's *The Crucible* at New York's Society for Ethical Culture, after which I was laid up with a three-week bout of mononucleosis. Claude was gone. He promised to write, but he didn't.

Instead, I found a note from Pastor Jerome Nathanson praising my performance with thanks. Enclosed was an invitation to the society's annual dinner, which I attended alone.

"Care to dance?" he asked.

I was mortified: "Thank you. I don't dance."

"Why not?"

"I don't like to."

"You don't like to?" he chided kindly. "How can you dislike such an obvious physical pleasure?"

I requested a private audience with him that week.

"Do you think it's wrong for a woman to go to bed with more than one man during the same time period?"

What woman? And why did I ask? At which I confessed my guilt.

"As well you should," he exclaimed. "If you didn't, you'd be morally insensitive." I said nothing. "What are your religious affiliations?"

"None."

He explained that Ethical Culture serves people who, with or without faith in God, believe in living the ethical life.

"The ethical life? What's that?" I asked. "I was a sinner before I became one. I've always felt that way."

"So why not enjoy it—is that it?" He looked carefully into my eyes. Was I in therapy? Not at present. Then he spoke of his friend, the psychiatrist Milton Sapirstein, author of *Paradoxes of*

Everyday Life.* He handed me a copy: "Read the chapter 'The Paradox of the Beautiful Woman.' And be warned," he said at the door: "Don't let him pawn you off on a colleague. He's your man."

According to Dr. Sapirstein, the beautiful woman's paradox lies in the terror of her charms, which so intimidate men, they hate her for them. That is why her less attractive sisters so often "beat her to the altar."

~

What was my problem? asked portly, bald, mustachioed Dr. Sapirstein.

Actually, I had more than one. I was dreadfully in love with Bob, but also with Claude. I lived with my widowed mother and made rounds every day for acting jobs—well, if not religiously, at least I went through the motions. "The fact is I'm miserable most of the time," I said cheerfully, because I was so happy to be there. But really, I didn't understand the source of so much pain. I'd had many affairs, but never a boyfriend; no man had ever kissed me on the lips. The year was 1956. I was twenty-two.

Dr. Sapirstein's diagnosis of me was swift and certain: "You're a girl in desperate need of a love situation." Just as Pastor Nathanson had predicted, he tried to send me to another doctor. No, I trusted *him*. Well, all right, he'd squeeze me in for twenty-five dollars a session. But I had a part-time receptionist's job that paid just that! He let me know it was below his usual rate; his other patients were prominent men. I never saw a woman among them.

At home, I'd record our talks in my diary. I wasn't about to forget what I signed over my salary for:

---

*Milton Sapirstein, *Paradoxes of Everyday Life* (New York: Random House, 1955).

"Look at you," he said, "you're an unsuccessful actress. You hop into bed with anyone you want, and you don't even tease them first to get them interested. You're an idiot."

I asked him what school of psychiatry he followed. "The reality school," he answered and, noting my confusion, added, "Don't you know who you are? You're a beautiful woman. Don't people look at you when you walk down the street?"

"Yes. So?"

"So you should be where my wife is! You should be where Teddy Newborn's wife is."

The producer Theodore A. Newborn, his former patient, was married to a working actress.

"A sweet girl," said Sapirstein, "but smart."

"And I'm dumb."

"Worse, you're a pretty girl who's an easy lay. No man has any respect for a woman unless she waits at least six to twelve dates before going to bed with him."

"Oh."

"Why do you do it? Afraid their penises'll fall off?"

"I find it hard to say no. I have needs, too."

"Nature girl!" he cried. "Do you always act on your needs? I'm a heavy man. If I ate all I wanted, I'd weigh four hun'-eighty pounds. Gimme one o' your cigarettes."

Serving him with cigarette and match, I swept gracefully back to my seat. Perhaps an exploration of my childhood might help clarify my behavior, I suggested. But my memory had not been sufficiently plowed to turn up more than a few bare facts that seemed to bore him. His eyes glazed over as he let me have my little say.

"Look, your childhood is over," he concluded, dousing his butt. "You came out of it retarded."

I wasn't insulted; his tone was affectionate. He'd mentioned more than once that his wife had had only sons; he wanted a daughter. And because I was young, he assumed it his duty to "marry me off." *Why* had I never had a boyfriend?

"Maybe I don't talk enough," I offered.

"You talk enough," he sighed.

But I had ideas! With everyone so eager to be slim, I could open a half-sandwich shop, where office workers could get their fill of protein on half the bread.

"Stick to your acting," he joked.

Lover Bob had gone back to his wife, and Luther to other conquests, when Dr. Sapirstein launched his first lecture on the vital importance of money: "You can have poor friends," he allowed. "Some of my best friends are poor. Jerome is poor. But *you* should be rich." Then, "I'm very corrupt," he added, puckishly lowering his gaze. "I like my patients to get ahead. And all you have to do is play games." Again I must have looked puzzled. "Hint at giving yourself," he explained, "*if* and *when*."

The next morning, Mother drew my attention to Dr. Fitzpatrick's name on the front page of the *New York Times*. Having dined at a friend's house, he'd said goodnight and hidden on the premises. Later, reentering the upstairs window from a ladder, he filled a knapsack with precious antiques and was spotted climbing down.

Why couldn't I respond to the tragedy of this kind man who had helped me? He was said to be suffering from kleptomania. His license revoked, he disappeared somewhere out West. I remembered his first private office—the odd little curios on his desk, and his comments on "certain Park Avenue psychiatrists." Dr. Sapirstein was of course among them. But Fitzpatrick had robbed his friends of precious objects for display; didn't that mark him a hypocrite? Sapirstein would be honestly "corrupt" on behalf of my best interests. *He* was my master now.

"How can anyone respect you?" he complained. "No one gives you anything! Don't you want anything? I have more respect for a grasping woman than I have for you. You're pathetic!" Finally, in a weary tone, "Why don't you give up the theater and look for something real?"

"My acting is real."

"You couldn't be content basking in some successful man's glory?"

"I'll kill myself first."

"It means that much?"

"It means that much."

When he pointed out that Mrs. Newborn's marriage to Teddy didn't exactly get in the way of her career, I agreed to marry a rich man with connections—but where was he?

"I have a patient in real estate," he said. "A super guy—I'm crazy about him. Backs Broadway shows. Connections at the best agencies—William Morris, MCA. If you're a good girl, I'll give him your number, he'll get them interested and then, if they like you, they'll sign you. Satisfied?"

It was said that at thirty-five, Henry Uffner owned Levittown. The millionaire "many times over" phoned next evening from his penthouse on Sixty-fifth and Park, where I was invited for Friday dinner. Mother was ecstatic. "This is from God," she said. "Your father's name was Henry."

"Whatever you do," warned Sapirstein, "don't sleep with him."

"Should I bring wine?"

"He doesn't need your wine."

But Mother said to bring it: "Show him you're his equal."

I nearly broke it tripping over his dog, Schlepper.

"Take it easy," said the slight, tawny-haired bachelor with a twinkle in his eye. "I'm Henry, by the way." Would I like a tour of the apartment while his butler was fixing dinner? I remember a fluffy, pale carpet, and huge rooms with French windows over-looking the surrounding terrace. His bed was oval, his bathtub square. At dinner he spoke readily about his accomplishments. Having quit college to pursue a business venture that led to his first million, he'd offered to send his mother to Europe. "First class," he emphasized, "but she didn't want to go; she'd rather sit home in the Bronx."

Afterward we strolled around the penthouse terrace discuss-ing our doctor: "What do you think of his book?" I asked.

"It was okay, though I never met the likes of any of his beau-tiful women. They don't intimidate *me*."

"Why should they?"

"You don't intimidate me!" he said.

"You don't intimidate me, either."

I leaned over the railing. A cool wind was blowing. He put his jacket around my shoulders. "Where do you spend your vaca-tions?" he asked.

"I don't take vacations."

"What do you do for a social life?"

"Not much," I admitted. "Usually I stay home and read."

He went out every night. "Milt thinks I have a marriage block, so I'm in therapy. But most girls are so boring," he sighed. "I hate it when they tease me and don't follow through."

"But to tease men is how we're trained! At least that's what Sapirstein's trying to teach me."

"How are you doing?" he joked.

"Not too well. It doesn't make sense! Either I'm attracted to someone or not, so I go to bed right away or not at all."

"Well, in that case . . . "

"You're not scared of me," he mused, dimming the lights.

"Why should I be? I trust you."

The next day, Dr. Sapirstein was furious. "You *are* an idiot," he concluded, "a sexually precocious idiot."

Why, because I couldn't say no? But that I should feel ashamed of what a man takes natural pride in made no sense! Nor did I understand why being beautiful was any credit to me. Why did Sapirstein think it was? That I might have slept with Henry to spite him, that I hated everything this pitiful thriver stood for, I never even knew. Of course I realized that unlike Dr. Fitzpatrick, Sapirstein made no effort to help me understand my problems. I simply assumed, as he did, that the right reality would cure me.

Or did he think me too stupid to profit from therapy? Well maybe I was. After all, he was a training analyst at Columbia. That my stupidity was an act, albeit an unconscious one, never entered his mind—or mine. Yet I could perceive at a glance, by his stomach-leading walk, his "Hell*ooo*" on the phone, Sapirstein's air of enterprise. Cock of the walk, he was teaching me success!

I had begun running a low-grade fever and coughing up blood, when Henry's friend Dr. Lou Scarrone checked me into New York Hospital for observation. There I was diagnosed with bronchitis and a mysterious, never-to-reappear injury to the heart muscle. I was also pregnant with Henry's child.

"Don't tell him," said Dr. Sapirstein, who had stopped by expressly to warn me: "I don't want it on his conscience."

"What about me?" I asked.

"I gave you a situation, and you acted like an idiot. Now get out of it by yourself."

Following my release from the hospital, where neither Dr.

Scarrone nor Henry bothered to visit, I had a second abortion. Sapirstein must have had an attack of conscience, or more likely feared "the idiot" might complain, because Henry phoned me afterward: Sapirstein had told him I was pregnant. If there was anything he could do to help . . . "Oh, no!" I interrupted. "After all, it's not as if it's *your* child!" At last I was angry! But I had remained loyal to Sapirstein, who shrewdly exonerated himself by blasting Dr. Scarrone for not visiting me: "He hospitalized you, didn't he? The cafe society doctor."

Henry invited me to rest up for the weekend at his West Hampton estate. There I found Scarrone with his date, an attractive model named Elaine. Henry's other guests included several major business tycoons who, like him, minored as theatrical angels. Their opinions at dinner on the worth of various Broadway box office hits prompted one of mine.

"Eat your scampi," someone responded.

Suddenly I didn't feel well; I went to my room to rest. Later, when Henry knocked on my door, I told him I felt sick. "Don't you believe me?" I asked, and for no reason, cried like a child.

"Come to my room," he said.

"So soon after . . . ?"

"Nothing'll happen," he assured.

When we were done: "Could I stay all night with you?" I asked.

"I think it's better if you go back to your room."

Sensible girl, I obeyed without question.

That night his friends shrieked under my window: "We want Carol! Where's Carol?"

∽

In late summer I heard that Theodore Newborn was producing a new Broadway musical. I introduced myself on the telephone as a patient of Dr. Sapirstein—the open sesame to success.

"I'm anxious to meet you," he said. "Why don't we make it semisocial?" His wife was in the country. Did I drink scotch?

"Are you pregnant again?" Sapirstein asked the next day.

Teddy had promised me a bit in his show.

I thought of Aliberti, how ashamed he'd be of me. Why, when I lost him, did I lose myself? Thoughts failed in the midst of remembering him that analytic hour, during which Sapirstein boasted of the confident women in his family who'd married well. How their little ones adored him: "Uncle Milt!" they'd shout. But he wouldn't hug them, not he: "I'm not a dirty old man." He recalled his student days at college when friends, seeing a woman decked out in furs, would mutter amongst themselves, "Disgusting ostentation," until *they* could afford them. He talked, I listened. I was there for him, not he for me. The sadder I got, the less I had to say or think.

When finally would I realize that I blamed myself merely for being? Conscience caused a weight in me no breath of air could lift. Guilty or not, I was guilty. My vital energies had been stunted. It was only a matter of time before a cancer of the spirit would consume them.

But not yet. A bit of success staved it off. Of my performance that summer in John Patrick's *Teahouse of the August Moon,* a reviewer wrote: "The entire production would be lost without the tenderly lyrical acting of Carol Hebald as the geisha girl. Her comedy, her self-choreographed dance, her delicate handling of the imaginary tea things, and her touching third act exit compare more than favorably with her Japanese predecessors on Broadway."

My dance! How did I think it up? I thought nothing. Then what happened to my tension problem? Nothing! My geisha costume hid my body. Kneeling on the floor, spine upright, neck and upper arms free, I simply embraced the music. I sent the review to Mother, who came to see the show with her new beau, Charles. On the arm of a man, she was happy again, and charming—so charming, she even praised me.

In the fall of '58 I was cast as the maid Leah in Huntington Hartford's Broadway adaptation of Charlotte Brontë's *Jane Eyre*. The show starred Errol Flynn as Rochester and Blanche Yurka as Mrs. Fairfax. Hartford imported an unknown British model for Jane. The out-of-town reviews were scathing. Flynn succeeded in getting out of his contract one freezing night in Cincinnati when, hearing a noisy off-stage boiler, he interrupted his final love scene with Jane to shout, "Who's knocking pipes back there, Mrs. Fairfax?" He was replaced first by John Emery, and finally by the British actor Eric Portman, whom I befriended at once. We opened in New York and lasted six weeks at the Belasco Theater.

On closing night, Helena Carroll called: She was playing Pegeen Mike in the Irish Players' production of Synge's *Playboy of the Western World*, but was having a fit of fatigue and needed a temporary replacement. Could I prepare her part in three days? Yes! It was a monumental task; I played for a month.

Despite my repeated invitations, Teddy Newborn wouldn't come to see me. Instead, after Helena's return, he gave me a pair of complimentary tickets to one of his shows, to which I invited a friend of Mr. Portman, a young actress named Vicky. Mother responded with such hysterical fury because I hadn't asked her, that she threatened to call Dr. Sapirstein.

"Tell on me to him, too, the way you told on me to Norman and Jani? Don't you want me to have any friends?"

"*I'm* your only friend," she hurled back. "Who feeds you? Who clothes you? Who takes care of you when you're sick?" I had no answer, except that I was leaving home for good. "Don't bother!" she replied. "I'm leaving you! I'm getting married before you!"

No sooner had Mother married Judge Charles Lifland and moved to Jersey City than she phoned to complain that her friends were blaming her for having abandoned me. Did she want my advice on handling them?

From as far back as I can remember, she'd warned Jan and me not to have children—and we didn't. Later, insisting she wanted me to marry, she did everything in her power to keep me home. Without a word, I hung up the phone. Having saved enough money to take myself to Europe for ten weeks, I sailed for London on the *Queen Elizabeth* in November 1958.

Chapter Nine

*E*mbarked on my first ocean voyage, I felt so painfully conspicuous I tried to distract myself by observing the couples around me: A fair, large-boned college girl who resembled a young Uta, traveling with her father; a honeymooning pair; and some pleasant old people. To those at my table who asked, I was an actress on a work-related trip. Returning quickly after meals to my cabin, I watched the waves from my porthole. What were my thoughts? At twenty-four, I felt betrayed by God. God *who?* In the twenty years that had passed since I'd put my father on His throne, had the devil himself crept up? Who *was* this two-personed, two-faced betrayer, powerless to pardon, eager to annihilate, whom I could appease only by acts of the most blatant self-sabotage?

Did I know the reputation I was getting? Didn't I realize my name was being passed around? Did I think my talent great enough to supersede it? Really, did I think at all? Or was I already "mad," insofar as I couldn't see that the toes I stepped on were mine? I didn't know it then, but my career was over. Despite my repeated invitations to agents, not one had come to see me in *Playboy.* Couldn't I have found some other way to suffer? Evidently not.

Entering the theater had been like entering a shrine. I was the kid who always arrived two hours early because I'd read somewhere that a great actor named Salvini did that, and I wanted to be just like him. For years Uta's classes had been central to that dream. But I rarely played for her anymore. Whatever I learned fell out from under me. She refused to criticize my work. Her comments to others, "You took a great leap forward there," or "You're conquering your problem with objects," were no longer addressed to me. Something was wrong, and she knew it. She was waiting for me to leave.

Sapirstein, too, had given up on me. His "therapy," which occupied itself with the fulfillment of my social needs, than which there was no greater goal, had left me out. I'd disobeyed him by sleeping with Henry; and again I hear his words: "I gave you a situation and you acted like an idiot. Now get out of it by yourself." Is this how successful men behave? Shortchange their discount (no-count?) clients because we get what we pay for, is that it? No wonder I held in contempt the very success I craved and did everything in my power to subvert it. Yet I was afraid to confront Sapirstein. When I tried: "Don't get upset with me," he warned. "*You're* the idiot." But he was the doctor. Was it so ridiculous to expect him to be human? More ridiculous still to make of him a god who gives audience only at fixed hours but seldom to the poor!

Why then did I long for his approval the same way I longed for Uta's? What should I go by, who follow? Didn't I know? Mute in their presence, I spoke eloquently in fantasy with them both. How long before I'd realize this very worst habit of dreamers? To imagine one's listener struck dumb, to plant on his cheek one small tear, saps the vital energy that might evoke that very response. This is the actor's nightmare. It was my nightmare in life.

I decided with all the extremism of youth that in Europe I'd let no one near me. I didn't want "to relate." Why should I force myself? What is the truth? I had needed so passionately and so often, I couldn't need anymore.

I should mention briefly that I had with me three prescription medications. Because the combination of a pill for my slow metabolism and an amphetamine to curb my appetite kept me awake, Sapirstein had prescribed the tranquilizer Miltown. Six a night did the trick. Resolved to cut back on these and as well to stop smoking, I spent the next ten weeks in virtual silence. I had come to teach my gaze outward, and this I did. I won't repeat the detailed accounts I kept of my first impressions of London, Paris, Vienna, and Florence. Arriving exhausted in Rome, I decided, despite my vow of isolation, to find my cousin Milton. Having recently won a Prix de Rome, he'd moved there with his wife, Cecille. Neither I nor my family had had any contact with him, or indeed with any other Hebald, since my father died. Only now does it strike me as odd that instead of checking at the American embassy or looking him up in the phone book, I searched along the streets and seacoast, asking total strangers, "Do you know the sculptor Milton Hebald?" My long weeks of self-imposed isolation had begun to take their toll.

I flew home on January 15. From Mother's old apartment, I wrote to Dr. Sapirstein asking him like a remorseful child to please take me back. He never responded. Instead, the psychologist Lee Salk, whom I'd met briefly at Henry's in West Hampton, called to invite me out. We agreed to meet at his place after his last patient had left. There I met his colleague, Dr. Broom.

"Very nice, I approve," he said of Lee's charming office-apartment.

"Not too pretentious?"

"No; refeeneed," joked Broom, thumb and forefinger circled in midair. The three of us were on our way to dinner when boyish Dr. Broom began cutting up spontaneously on the street. I joined him in hallooing out loud.

"Shhhhh," admonished Lee. "If any of my patients should see me!"

"You have all the characteristics of the youngest child," began Jonas Salk's baby brother when finally we were alone. A slight, balding young wizard, Lee did not attract me, so we spent our few dates talking. He referred often, though anonymously, to his patients. The story of one, who was making great strides in her relationship with her possessive mother, permitted me to speak of mine. In addition, I told Lee how my compulsive eating binges led to depressions that interfered with my acting. I admitted that acting was more important to me than life. I'd give it up for no one.

Here are his responses, as recorded in my January 1959 diary. They must have occurred over a period of weeks. I include them not as criticism of Lee, who at thirty was just starting out, but as an illustration of the conventional wisdom of the time on "neurotic" career women.

First, I was terrified of sex. This I attributed to my rejection of his advances. But why did he think so? I asked. "Because sex leads to pregnancy, and the only reason you haven't reared a house full of children by now is that you're afraid they'll hate you as much as you hate your mother."

Next: "Your food binges fill a need for a father and babies. Each time you overeat you're experiencing an immaculate conception. That you won't give up the theater for any man is a lie. You don't want the theater, though you probably have talent."

"Thank you very much," I replied.

"You have no courage," he taunted playfully, poking me.

"What do you mean?"

"Get yourself a good Freudian analyst. Your acting is a defense."

What did this upstart know of my work? For spite, I lit into his: "I don't know where you get your theories or why you think they apply to me. But if this is an example of good Freudian analysis, I'd as soon see a priest."

"No, you wouldn't."

"Oh? Why not?"

"The priest comforts, the analyst helps you understand," he touted.

"Understand what? Injustice? Maybe I'd like to *do* something about unfair conditions."

"What unfair conditions?"

"I don't understand why 'certain Park Avenue psychiatrists' can't live just as well on Lexington. It's bad enough we can't bill the people who made us sick. We should at least pay according to our means. All other professions have unions, minimum rage laws . . . "

"Rage laws?"

I suppose I laughed, too, but I was dead serious. He said of course things were wrong with the world, but he couldn't change them. Worse, my desire to do so to suit my own ends was symptomatic of my neurotic, infantile behavior.

I listened with interest as he rattled on about professional women: All nurses have mean mothers. The mean nurses "become" them; the nice ones "sublimate" by kind-mothering their patients. Spinster schoolteachers all "make the transference" by saying "my children"; masturbation is terrible to them because they indulge in it so much. Finally, I intellectualized and analyzed too much.

"I?"

Well, at least Lee talked to me. He would be one of many—some lovers, some not—who in the process of advising poor Carol revealed themselves and the mental fashions of the time.

One lonely Friday night in February, I admitted to my diary

that I might not succeed in the theater. I'd gained much weight and, refusing to shed my coat in public, had that day poked my head in an agent's door, mumbling, "You don't need me today, do you?" I wrote of my longing for the side streets of Europe: If I were an author, I could travel around on royalties and never have to see or speak with anyone again. But an author of what?

I found a modest studio apartment in a walk-up on East Seventy-seventh Street. Jan said it resembled a prison cell, but I loved it—a long, narrow room with a high barred window revealing a patch of sky. On the sill I placed an old quill pen and inkwell. Adjoining the bath was a little square dressing room where, under another high window, I put a typewriter and chair. There, a few months later, I would write my first short story.

In the meantime, I'd kept in touch with Eric Portman's friend Vicky, who gave me the name of a psychiatrist formerly recommended to her.

~

On Feb. 21, 1959, I had my first session with Dr. Martin Zohrman, whose office was six short blocks from my apartment. I fantasized immediately that I'd be visiting my father twice a week— Wednesdays and Saturdays at 10:10 A.M. He'd be my doctor for the next six years.

As with Dr. Sapirstein, I'd pay a special fee: twenty dollars a session. But, oh, the difference between them—beginning with Zohrman's modest bearing, his light Virginian accent, and his immaculate suits and ties. He wore a crewcut, had a square jaw, and was short and hefty like my father. No more than thirty-five, he looked a good deal older. He wrote steadily all through our first interview. I was telling him about Mother's presence at my new apartment to cosign the lease. The landlord had asked me a question that she answered for me. When I burst out at the memory, "Let me talk!" the tears welled up so painfully he stopped writing and looked at me. His very soul was in his eyes. Transference or love at first sight, I felt an intimacy so sudden, I assumed its speed a measure of my hunger and, from shame, kept it to myself. Instead, recalling Lee Salk's frequent references to transference, I asked Dr. Zohrman what it meant. He defined it simply as our endowment of the therapist with the characteristics of our earliest caregivers. He would in time represent—that is, *become* in my unconscious mind—my father, mother, sister, and Barbara. I then asked what he expected of me. His answer: the realization that my yet-to-be-expressed infantile responses to him—whether excessively submissive or rebellious (they had to be excessively *something*)—were inappropriate in my present circumstances. The object being to "work through" my past, these responses were to be valued as clear indicators of my problems with others.

"Is there any homework I can do?" I asked in a hushed tone at the door.

"No," he answered with a smile.

Yet despite myself (to spite myself?) I plan to impress him, without seeming to do so: All spear carriers are *not* erect, I'll put in casually. And just in case he might be subject to other current misconceptions—some *awfully* intelligent people were—such as, for example, all career women are neurotic, or all whores common, I'll clarify that although I've been promiscuous, I'm vulnerable, shy, and, above all, an artist. I was merely trying on a role distant from my nature. Well, wasn't that partially true? Sometimes we grasp the truth too quickly to credit it, I'll say, because it sounds erudite. I make a formal list of problems (because I'm paying for every word). Soon I'll come to love him so much I'll tell my diary things I can't possibly say to him. For now:

1) Discuss how easily lies leap out of your mouth. Vow to catch yourself, always, in the act of tripping yourself up. (He'll have to keep you on then.)

2) To help him get to know you as an artist, discuss acting; show him *Teahouse* reviews.

3) Cover early life: the three Furies—Jan, Barbara, Mother.

4) Admit feelings of attraction for him, my immense shame over having given my body to others so freely, and my fear that he'll send me to another doctor.

5) Tell all that happened with Dr. Sapirstein.

FEBRUARY 28, 1959

I covered my list in ten minutes flat.

His response: "You talk about your feelings *without* your feelings." That was, of course, because I'd prepared. "Don't prepare anything," he repeated. "Preparation for sessions is a common defense mechanism." Against what? Spontaneous behavior. "People facing situations that cause them anxiety tend to detach themselves."

"May I write that down?"

He shrugged. Then, "What do you do all day?"

"I make rounds."

"All day?"

"All day."

He warned that therapy would do me no good unless I had a specific goal, a point of orientation. "My other patients have jobs or marriages from which they get fired or rejected. You've got neither."

"I'm making rounds for acting jobs," I answered a bit tartly, "and given the state of the American theater, it isn't my fault I'm unemployed." He asked if it was in acting I should stay. "Look, there's no need to question the one area of my life I'm not ambivalent about," I said.

"Are you sure?" he asked, jotting something down, and before I could answer warned, "Don't rush into any decisions," his free hand shooting up for emphasis.

"Don't worry, I won't! I'll get a night job waiting tables at Riker's if that'll help you, but I'll continue making rounds during the day." Then, more humbly, "Is that all right?"

"If I told you what to do, I'd be a counselor, not a therapist."

MARCH 3

"What do you want in a relationship?" he began.

"I want someone to take care of me and make me great."

He smiled. "You want a great deal."

"Too much?"

"I think you expect too much of yourself." Then, "If you expected less of yourself, people would like you better."

I'm sure.

But the problem is to find that "point of orientation" he can work from. I should let him do his job. But how? Fail at a relationship because that's what he's in the business of repairing?

MARCH 9

Today I expressed confusion about some of the blank spaces in my childhood: "I'd really like to know the connection between my sexual encounters in the movies and my wanting to be an actress."

"You would, and you wouldn't," he mused, cocking his head in thought.

"What do you mean?"

"You don't want answers. They interfere with the fantasies you have about yourself."

"What fantasies?"

"I don't know. I've only seen glimpses of them. But they play a poor second to your facts."

"How can you know that when you don't know what they are?"

"I don't."

"How do you know I *have* fantasies?"

"Because we all have them."

"What makes you so sure mine are worse than yours?"

"I'm not."

"Then why am I sicker than you?"

"I don't know that you are!"

MARCH 12

"What is my reality?" I asked him smartly.

"That your needs can't be filled. There's no way at your age you're going to find a mother and father. You'll always be disappointed. And if you continue to retreat into fantasies, you'll never be any happier than you are now."

I live in one world, and he defines its boundaries from another. Though yesterday, when he admitted presenting me with suppositions that, depending on my responses, he either drops or follows up, I leapt with delight into his: "That's like Stanislavsky's method of improvisation," I cried, "to bring actors closer to their characters. Did you know that Freud and Stanislavsky were contemporaries, and that our sense memory exercises are based on Pavlov's theory of conditioned response?"

But he wasn't pleased to hear my ideas. I should concentrate on my ambivalence. So I told him that my real aim, to get him to love me, is at odds with my declared aim, to get well.*

"How so?"

"Because the objectives conflict: I'd rather arouse your sympathy than work through the situations of my childhood."

He threw up his hands in impatience. He's trying so hard, and getting such a thin time of it from me. Rising to sum up the hour, he announced, "You're not looking for a father in a man, but for a better mother." What I'm supposed to do with that piece of information, I don't know. That I prefer my needs to their satisfaction he rejects entirely; he doesn't understand it. I think he thinks I argue too much.

MARCH 20

I learned today through Vicky that he is married: "Very married," said a doctor friend of hers, whom she'd asked on my behalf. "You can relay the message," he added. "Zohrman's wife is my patient."

I am devastated. Now, wherever I walk I imagine Dr. Zohrman watching over me. I want to be the older sister of his unborn child. I have to be careful. If he knows the extent of my feelings, he'll send me to someone else.

Resolving to admit them anyway, thinking he'd praise my courage, I told him also that although I haven't worked since my return from Europe—a mere three months—I am stopped on the street by fellow actors who say, "I heard you were wonderful in *Playboy.*" "They're flattering me, of course," I hastened to add. "The greatest unconscious genius couldn't have been wonderful

---

*My use of the terms *real* and *declared aims* is borrowed from George Orwell's essay "Politics and the English Language," in *Shooting an Elephant and Other Essays* (New York: Harcourt, Brace, 1950).

given three days to prepare a role as difficult as Pegeen Mike."
Then I concluded, despite his sigh of impatience, "I was simply
surprisingly good under the circumstances." He has to know I'm
a respected professional, and a modest one at that, so he'll dis-
miss from his mind the very possibility I'd ever give up acting.

Then why am I doing less and less about getting a job? Sometimes I feel too unhappy to leave the house. I'm waging a terrific
battle over this. *Am* I ambivalent about acting? No, goddammit!
Do I have to make him right about everything? I can't decide
whether he's unmasked a real conflict or I'm manufacturing it to
appease him.

I'm still furnishing my new apartment. His consulting room
and my studio share the same rectangular shape. Though I speak
with him in session from an upright chair, the black daybed on
which I sleep will occupy the same relative space as his blue analytic couch. I even place my chairs in a similar arrangement to
his, the box of Kleenex at my side. Now I am with him always in
my imagination.

I wait at home for his visit. I sit in my wing chair; he, diagonally opposite, in my armchair. He is reading; I am writing. Each
time I look up his eyes are on me with an expression of infinite
love.

Fact: He never said he'd come. He never did.

Chapter Ten

*D*r. Zohrman admitted he hasn't had many patients who were locked in closets before they were one year old, only to have the experience recur later in childhood. What's his point? I must have screamed to go into the closet, where my fantasies had free reign. I suggested that if my illness began there so too did my creative life, that there was a purpose for my pain, and he wrote this down.

He went on: Because I grew up thinking I should be punished for wanting love, my fantasy now is to put others in closets. I agreed to be my sister's slave because at least she talked to me. But later in school, I *became* her. And there my troubles began.

I became Jani? He was improvising again and I permitted it because I don't want him to think I'm defensive. But really, when did I ever order others about or threaten people like Jani, who, by the way, is always sweet in company, whereas I . . . Well, there may be things I don't remember.

APRIL 10

"You're filled with guilt," he offered this morning.

"It's true," I confessed. "Still, I want people to see me naked, physically and emotionally."

"There's a great deal of exhibitionism in your behavior."

"Is that bad?" I asked, like a little girl.

"Good or bad is not the question!"

I lowered my head. "I'm guilty I think . . . because of the abortions."

"Do you know how many millions of women have abortions every year?" As though my conscience were at fault, and not I.

"I don't sit in judgment of them."

"Oh, no? What makes you different? You think you're better than everyone else and that makes you contemptib . . . contemptuous of them."

Pause. "You meant contemptible."

"No, I didn't."

"Verbal slips apply to me and not to you?"

He picked some lint off his trousers, let the moment pass. Had he asked why I considered myself superior to others, I couldn't have told him. I can't word the thought, but something in me knows that to call an action right because many people engage in it is dumb.

APRIL 14

"What's vital to your recovery is to get angry at the people who hurt you," he stressed this morning. "Don't you ever want to shout, 'those bastards! I'll tell them where to get off at!' You can understand feelings only by reliving them. That's what is meant by *working through,* so you can accept your hatred and stop doing penance over it." Finally, "Unless you get angry with me, you'll never be able to relate."

I'm terribly insulted. I want him to think I'm lovely, and all he sees is rage. He's trying to pump it out of me ("You certainly *are* an angry woman") and, when he fails, faults me for not trying. Love and hate are wavering so painfully inside me, I don't know how to try, but instead imagine for hours on end my "Who's there?" at the door, his welcome into my room, the way I set down his tea.

APRIL 20

"You know, society punishes us for what we do; we punish ourselves for what we *want* to do."

"My family . . . they were sick, too, very sick to have been so mean."

"When you believe that, you'll be internally cured."

At the door: "My rage was never expressed; it turned inside?" I asked, like the sweet-slow child I think he loves.

APRIL 24

"Your feelings are intolerable." This I could not deny. We sat silent until it was time to go. When I rose, he asked where I was off to; and when I answered, "To a singing audition," he exclaimed, "You can barely talk! How can you sing?" He'd have been surprised.

MAY 1

Finally I admitted he's with me all the time, that I can't stop thinking about him. He replied that he wants our relationship to be on as realistic a basis as possible. His dilemma is clear: How to treat a patient who won't budge? But when I explained I don't do better because I don't *want* to do better, since getting well would mean losing him, he asked where I thought my feelings for him could lead. I couldn't answer that, but in the remaining silence felt his approval, and at moments an exquisite understanding that bordered on love.

MAY 8

"What do you think your worst problem is?" he asked.

"My weight," I said, because I can't control my eating binges and have yet to shed my coat in his office.

"Your weight!" he replied, amazed, because though I feel fat, starvation diets keep my weight within normal range.

"What do *you* think it is?" I asked.

"I think you can't distinguish fact from fantasy. It must be very hard for you to distinguish between who you are, what you want to be, what you're afraid of being, what you think you are, and what you imagine others think of you." He took a deep breath; then summing up, warned me not to be overwhelmed: "It's true of everyone. It's just a question of degree."

But if *he* can't distinguish between my facts and fantasies, and I don't know where the line exists . . . Of course, I do know but hesitate to contradict him. The more I stifle my objections, the less I trust them.

MAY 13

"And your pain and anger kept adding up until your fantasy of being God's special child slipped into your unconscious. You think one fine day He'll help you destroy the world. You believe your anger has magic power, but you're wrong." Then very gently, "And you're wrong about there being a purpose for the pain. There *is* none."

I hate it when he gets gentle. It feels like he's playing with his power.

That night I remembered my father masturbating in his bed, saying to me, "Come a little closer."

I phoned Dr. Zohrman in terror. He saw me next day.

When I confronted the memory more calmly, I recalled not fear, but the most intense pleasure I'd ever known.

"Is it true?" I asked him. "Do you think it happened?"

"It's not the fantasy or memory itself that's important," he answered. "All little girls have sex fantasies about their fathers."

"But if I don't know if mine is true?"

"Does it feel true?"

"Yes."

I was overcome with nausea; he told me to try to control it.

At home I admit wanting it to be true because it brings me closer to my father. And the scenario itself is so moving! Think, I tell myself: from the clothes in the closet, to the men in the movies, to an audience in the theater. To act, I have to act—to wish by a director's order, behave according to a playwright's plan. And couldn't I be the playwright too? I was so struck by my fictional possibilities that I wrote my first short story—about a little girl who imagines knocking on the gate of heaven, where she thinks her father is. But wouldn't God have sent my father to hell for what he did? Oh, no! He was in terrible pain. If I understand that, how can't God?

MAY 17

In session today: "And just because I want it to have occurred - doesn't mean it didn't," I argued.

"On the contrary, your making a story of it is a defense against the probability of it having occurred."

"Then you think it did?" He shrugged his shoulders. "Is it bad to see my past in stories?"

"Good or bad is not the question! What else do you remember?"

Specific incidents resurface both in his office and at home. Am I unnatural for feeling such intense pleasure at the memories?

"At three or four? You can't *get* much sexier."

At which I admitted I want it to have occurred also because it makes me different.

"You're not so different," he countered. "I think you like to think you are."

Always when I tell the truth I get smacked in the face.

Memories of my father continue to rush back. His words, "Close your eyes and open your mouth." Is he giving me candy, or . . . ? "Take down your pants." Is he giving me a spanking, or . . . ? Well, did it happen? Didn't it happen? Did I want it to happen?—Oh, yes. More and more. I'm sinking back into childhood, and I can't lift myself out. It's getting harder and harder to leave the house.

"Your isolation is automatic," cautioned Zohrman. "You have to fight it, do you understand?"

He's telling me what to do, "like a counselor," and I like that. I want him also to tell me what to wear, how to fix my hair, and what to eat for breakfast.

Today I asked, how wise is it to discourage my warm feelings for him, the first nice heterosexual man toward whom I've ever had such feelings? I was quick to add that though I wanted him to share them, if he ever acted on them I'd lose all respect for him: "I want you to *want* me; I don't want you to *take* me." He looked worried; so I drew myself up tall. "In fact, my problem of running from the attainable to the impossible should be one of the things we concern ourselves with in this office." I expected him to applaud.

Instead, "There's no reason why you shouldn't have warm feelings for me—or I for you. If you slimmed down and took your coat off, I might very well want to go to bed with you. But I'm not going to because I'm your doctor." He said I may have distorted his question about where our relationship could lead: "All I meant is that you should talk about real things."

"Dates?" He nodded. "But you know I don't want them."

"I think you're ashamed of wanting them. You're ashamed of

all your needs. One of the ways you can shed that shame is by expressing your fantasies about me."

~

I was applauded in acting class for my performance as the meek daughter Alexandra who finally stands up to her cruel mother in Lillian Hellman's *The Little Foxes*. Said the teacher, "I don't know how you get those results."

"Well, it's no trick," I answered. "I just chose the right obstacle to Alexandra's telling her mother off."

"Well?"

"Her love for her, of course."

"Ah!" breathed out the class. I was happy again. All I have to do is work well, and my problems disappear.

MAY 18

"I have no illusions about creating anything exciting in the American theater," I announced happily. "I know it beyond a shadow of a doubt."

"So the whole American theater depends on you," jabbed Zohrman.

"Don't worry, it will," I said coolly.

"Why are you angry?"

Because he unfairly provoked me. Behavior-modificating motherfucker! Is this what's known as testing patient threshold? Can't he allow me a little pleasure over a classroom success?

"Why?" he had the dumb nerve to repeat.

MAY 24

I brought him my story, which he took twenty minutes to read. He seemed involved. I stared at the pictures on his wall so he could get more involved. Finished, he looked up, quiet, pale. I noticed a slight tinge of purple along the delicate veins of his eyelids. Is it possible I made him cry?

"Did you like it?" I asked stupidly.

"It scans . . . beautifully. I see the child, as though she herself is talking. It's deeply moving."

I'm in ecstasy. The next time, I showed him my two poems. Without a word he handed them back. The proud smile on his face told me everything.

"You think I could be a writer?"

"I do," he said sincerely.

And he wonders that I adore him. He is the giver, I the taker. That I should be worthy of his gifts is my most obedient hope. He fertilizes my mind, makes thoughts blossom. Now they're sprouting like unruly plants. I want him to be my doctor forever and ever and ever. I'm going to write a play called *Transferential Follies of 1959*. What's happening? I can't leave his praise alone, but reread my story through his eyes, making sure the words are rightly placed, then, before I know it, relive the events that shaped them. My mind chews the cud of memory, all that might have been, and the slow fading of my strength from disappointment, outrage from too much pain. I don't want to live anymore.

MAY 26

"Why am I here?" I asked, again a child.

"Better relationships." That sounded so silly. "Your need for love is enormous," he went on, "and you don't know how to ask for it." Ask for love? I cringed at the thought.

Still, "Where do I begin? Where do I express . . . ?"

"You do that here," he declared emphatically.

But whenever I try, he tells me my energies are in fantasy. Then he encourages me to say whatever comes into my mind, and in the next breath complains I don't stick to any one particular thing. How can I hook my thoughts to one wagon train at a time when the tracks keep crossing?

He looks sadder and sadder to me. The phrase "gorgeous aching hunger" recurs over and over in my diary. I'm too excited to sleep; I gorge all night on sweets. He gives me two prescriptions: one for the amphetamine Dexamil to curb my appetite, the other for the tranquilizer Compazine (20 milligrams a day) to counteract anxiety. My feelings are "too intense." Last week, when he opened his drawer to give me samples, I felt as though my daddy were giving me candy: Papa's milk in sugarcoated pills that put me to sleep in his arms.

He'd like to know the meaning of the things I "spew out"; my thoughts and feelings are "disorganized." I have to have them "simplified."

"Where are you?" he asked finally when our time was up. Wanting only to speak. Only to be able to speak.

~⋅∽

Eric Portman had invited me to his party at the Dakota, where my friend Vicky came with her new beau, Denis. "He's going to want you," she had warned me. "Stay away from him."

But it was a long evening and Denis, seeing me alone, asked who I was. I told him, then excused myself. On my way to the rest room, Vicky cornered me: "I don't trust you," she whispered, "even though you're my dearest friend."

"I'm sorry you feel that way," I said, and a few minutes later decided to leave. I went to Eric's bedroom for my coat, and finding Vicky on the phone with her mother, was tipsy enough to collapse into an armchair and give way to a bath of sobs: "I want my daddy. Where's my daddy?" Alarmed, Vicky hung up and called Eric into the room.

"What's the matter?" he asked, kneeling at my side. "Is there something you want you can't have?"

"My daddy," I cried uncontrollably.

"Where *is* your daddy?"

"He's gone."

"Then he can't very well be here, can he? But look at all the advantages you have."

The next day, Zohrman beamed with pleasure: "It's good to express a need, isn't it, and then feel better for it?"

At the time, yes. But I don't think it could have done my career much good to regress in public. Especially since Vicky called to relay that when I told Eric my daddy was gone, he wondered, to Westchester or the world beyond?

MAY 26

"Acting is your greatest defense," said Zohrman today.

"Is it a good one?"

"If you're successful." Then, "You want so many things and you don't do anything about them."

"Ever since the *Island of Goats* episode, I lost all courage." I relayed the story of my four auditions.

"Did you *do* it?" he asked.

"Do what? I just told you. I went to the opening and . . ."

"Did you *do* it?"

"No! They kept the original actress. She was blonde; Uta was blonde. They made me try it so many ways. Could I make her a little gentler here, a little less angry there?"

"They thought you were too angry?"

"I was trying different interpretations!"

"So the whole American theater depends on you."

That night I took an overdose of sleeping pills. Zohrman phoned to change an appointment. An ambulance took me to the hospital, where I had my stomach pumped. At our next session he wanted to know what upset me so much. That I wasn't good for the part?

"Good for the part? They said they were electrified. Why did you ask me twice, 'Did you do it?' You were pushing my face into a memory the way Barbara used to . . . "

"I wanted to know if you did it."

He wasn't listening!

Again, "Why did you overdose?"

"Because I wanted to take your pride away as a doctor."

There was hatred for me on his face as he summed up the hour: "You blamed yourself for your father's death and you've been killing men ever since."

"Men have been taking advantage of me all my life and *I* kill *them?* What are you talking about?"

"You did it with me."

"I don't understand!"

"You did it with me."

What does that prove? Nothing but the all-patients-reenact-with-their-therapists theory he parrots as though he invented it. He is doing violence to my reality for the sake of theory!

I have a series of terrifying dreams that expose me as a criminal. I think Zohrman is treating me like one, but doesn't know it. I may be wrong, but I know I'm right.

And in the midst of all this, I confess to my diary that I want to get married because if I don't, people will think something's wrong with me.

Chapter Eleven

*I*t's summer, 1959. Walt Witcover has hired me as resident ingenue at the Crystal Lake Lodge Resort in Chestertown, New York, where I'm playing Laura in Williams's *Glass Menagerie*, Cleo in Odets's *Rocket to the Moon*, and Juliet in Anouilh's *Thieves' Carnival*. I'm working extremely well. Audiences say that they can't recognize me from one play to the next, so completely do I take them with me each time.

But our entire company is disturbed because we don't have separate dining arrangements. Neither does the band. Like them, we're expected to disperse and join the guests. Can't we eat alone before performances? No, but not to worry. Although the Crystal Lake brochure advertises "dine with live actors" (as opposed to dead ones?), we're not obliged to make small talk. I speak only when spoken to, except with Freddy the bass player, a sad, fat man of forty-four who follows me around and asked today at lunch why I've been avoiding him.

When I'm not rehearsing, I can join the guests swimming or lounging at the lake house. Instead I've filled 386 pages with thoughts about Zohrman. I fantasize that he and his wife are vacationing at nearby Lake George and that he steals off to watch me wherever I go. Among the guests are several doctors, whom I imagine he has sent to spy on me.

AUGUST 16

A couple of nights ago, after the show, I made love with Freddy. "Now you're my chick," he said.

He's nineteen years my senior (as my father was my mother's), and I'm comfortable with him because he's fat. But I hate it when he bosses me around. It was pouring this morning when he asked me out. I told him I wanted to read, write, and wash clothes.

"Wash your clothes on a sunny day," he said.

"No."

"Again no?" He wouldn't talk to me at dinner.

AUGUST 23

On my day off I traveled in to Manhattan to see Zohrman, who's back from vacation, suntanned and smiling. Has his wife given birth? When I told him the audience's praise of my work, I added, "I think you don't believe me."

"Not only do I believe you," he said, "I think it's very well deserved."

Then he *did* come to see me? I don't dare ask, but inspired by gratitude, plan on my bus trip back to share a wonderful question that popped up when he was away: To what extent did my "downfall" occur as a result of sympathy for my oppressors? I mull it over for several days; it doesn't yield an answer. Instead, the idea looms to rewrite "Cinderella" with mercy for the mean, ugly stepsisters.

"'Cinderella' is an immoral story," I declared the following week, "because it teaches that pretty women are good and unattractive ones bad. Her ugly stepsisters felt shortchanged because they were! But wouldn't any kid wonder: shortchanged because they were evil, or evil because they were shortchanged? They had reason to be angry with Cinderella just as Jani and Barbara had reason to be angry with me for being pretty. They beat me and locked me up, not for my own good, but to get me out of the way."

Zohrman looked happy.

"And Prince Charming—what a schmuck. Excuse me! But what a way to choose a wife: 'Does *your* foot fit? How about *yours?*' Couldn't he have loved her with normal feet? Why should all princes be charming and all orphans skinny?"

"I don't know." He smiled.

"I'm not wrong," I persisted. "There *is* a purpose for the pain."

"How's that?"

"Because if I had a healthy mother and father, I might be intelligent enough to concede that 'Cinderella' is a demoralizing piece of horseshit, but I wouldn't feel strongly enough to change it. I'd make her ugly with fat legs and big, smelly feet, and the mean sisters pretty; let Cinderella be the old maid who finds another place for herself in the world!"

He looked proud: "I don't know if you'll make it in the theater," he said, "but you'll make it somewhere."

I was beaming inside—too happy to look at him. But then everything changed when I mentioned Freddy: "He loves me— he said so." Zohrman smiled broadly. I looked away. "I'd better break it off," I muttered.

"Why?" I shook my head. "You go so far in a relationship and no further."

"Why are they so hard for me?"

"Why? . . . "

All week I've been balking at my supposed wish to destroy the world. It's not an airtight interpretation, he assures. He's still testing his theories by my responses. What does he expect me to do?

Do I deny his "interpretation" because it's true or because, being false, it's blatantly unfair? It's logical, isn't it, that given the opportunity, victims will victimize ("You want to put others in closets"), but does that make it universally so? Zohrman himself said,

"You can follow a perfect line of logic and be totally divorced from reality."

The final week at Crystal Lake Freddy accuses me unjustly of having an affair with a fellow actor. Now I have reason to be rid of him for good.

SEPTEMBER 10

I'm back in New York with no job, no prospects. Everything fresh has dried up in me. I can't rewrite "Cinderella." I'm so far off, twirling in the darkness, I don't know where to begin.

"Only a few weeks ago onstage I knew who I was, I had a place to behave."

"You have a life to live," pressed Zohrman.

"I don't want it." It slipped out; he knew I meant it.

"You've been expressing a death wish ever since you came here, and it's only your anger."

It seems I'd rather die than work through it. He said I make *him* angry; that all my life my mother and sister have been tearing me down, and I think he's doing the same. "But I'm not," he insisted. "Not only do I believe in your talent, I think you're an extremely bright and perceptive woman."

He's trying to regain my trust because he's afraid I'll kill myself. But he can't hide his contempt for me, any more than I can hide my rage from him.

"You give a starving child a small bite of food, you make her realize how hungry she is," I said.

"What are you feeling right now?"

"I want to sleep in your arms but I'd rather smash your face in than hold your hand."

"Pretty ambivalent feelings," he remarked expectantly.

Feelings again, always feelings rush-rush-rushing to erupt, only to shut off like a faulty tap. "You're not trying," he prodded; and "Do you believe in magic?"

I could barely hold my head up, and he kept punching away . . . punching away . . .

"What is it?" he asked quietly. Something strangled the words in my throat. "Say it!"

"Punching away . . . " And then it came back: how after my father died, I used to sneak out of the house to find my mother. "I'd get lost. Once I almost got run over. A stranger brought me home. That night, Mother tried to make me promise never to cross the street alone. I wouldn't—for spite. She didn't know what to do.

" 'Force her!' cried Jan. And they shoved me up against the wall and hit me."

"Did you promise?" asked Zohrman.

"No."

A pause. "Was that why Barbara locked you in closets? Because if it was, they might have known. They might have consented to it for your safety."

"But Barbara said she'd kill me if I told."

"Because they weren't supposed to know. On the other hand, maybe they didn't. What's the matter?"

"They took turns hitting me for something else. Before my father died, I told them how he touched me. He said not to, but I did. Later I walked into his room. He was all yellow with cancer; he had no strength. "Child, what have they done to you?" was all he said.

SEPTEMBER 14

I relayed a dream: I'm three years old, alone with my father in his room. "Get me my medicine," he says. But I just stand there.

"Can one dream a memory?" I asked. Zohrman doesn't know.

I'm slipping backward; I don't have much further to go. Memories again overwhelm me. Zohrman is "very concerned." Why? I thought he wanted me to relive them; that there's no understanding them otherwise! I don't know what he wants from me. I don't know what understanding means!

He suggested there's an area of my life I haven't told him about.

"Perhaps if I lie on the couch and have a formal analysis . . ."

"Any doctor who'd do a formal analysis with you outside of a hospital would be crazy."

"What about group therapy?"

"It's not for you." Pause. Again he stabs me with the question: "How do you feel about me?"

"Why should I tell you? I have my answer."

"You can't possibly think of a third alternative, can you?"

My nightmares won't let up. I warn him not to push me too far.

OCTOBER 12

"What are you thinking?" asked Zohrman, after a long silence.

"That I can't face never seeing you again after treatment."

"You don't have to face it yet."

"If I just . . . had a place in your thoughts."

"You have it," he said quickly. I looked up. "Why is it so important?"

"I'm afraid you'll leave me wide open and disappear, just like my father."

"That's because you see men only as sex objects. You don't think they can give you anything more."

"That's not true!" I objected. "It's the men I chose."

NOVEMBER 9

"You know other girls of four lose their fathers."

He wanted to know what happened with mine, and reaching for his clipboard, averted his eyes.

"I lay on my back across his stomach. He wouldn't let me see his face. I wanted to turn around, but he wouldn't let me."

"I think you feel pain telling me this," he prompted.

"In the movies, I wanted to be taken into the men's laps. Men have asked why I cry during sex. I couldn't tell them, I want to love them, and they won't let me. 'What's the matter?' they'd ask. 'Am I hurting you?' There's pain in my throat—pain and ecstasy in my stomach, breasts, and throat."

"What did your father do?"

"He played with me and moved his body . . . the gestures of intercourse." I felt tense describing it. I made an effort to relax; the words I said were true, but my feelings were absent.

He pressed me again for fantasies about him. I said dully, "My head is on your chest," or "I can't fall asleep unless you're holding me." I squirmed from shame when he responded, "That's very nice."

NOVEMBER 12

I walked into his office smiling. I don't know why I couldn't stop.

"Do you know what's happening?" he asked, his brows knit deeply in concern. "You're regressing."

"What's that?"

"Relapsing into childhood. You look dazed."

"Oh."

Is that why he's been so sweet to me? He's concerned that my wish to die is stronger than my wish to live.

"When I admitted the possibility of failure in the theater, I gave up all hope of success," I explained.

He said part of my present unhappiness is because I realize I want more than acting. I admit I do. I want to please him, to make myself welcome again in his thoughts. "It would be good to give and take something of importance and meaning," I added.

"I wonder if you're not talking about love."

"Yes, I imagine I am."

"I wonder if you're not talking about marriage."

"I don't know if I am or not. Maybe I am."

"It's very painful, I know," he affirmed. "But it's part of your progress in getting well. Mating is an instinct, a need."

"Why don't some people ever marry?" I asked.

"Previous painful experience," he answered simply. "You know in reliving things, the purpose is not only to feel, but to understand your feelings."

To feel so as to understand? But the more I feel, the more preposterous it seems to have to relive everything in order to realize that my rage is justified. And then what? Join the human race I'm supposed to want to destroy?

"At least the bastards treated me badly. You nice ones didn't treat me at all."

"Why didn't they like you?"

"Because I wasn't well-groomed or well-dressed. Because I wasn't clean. Because I answered back my teachers. Because I was stupid and couldn't concentrate. Because nobody taught me manners. Because I had nobody to be like. But I didn't harm anyone! I just wanted someone to play with. I guess I'm pretty angry. I've never been angry like this."

"Not before today."

"Was I that unattractive as a child?"

"Then you weren't much."

"And now?"

"Oh, you can go to the top of the ladder now." I covered my face from joy. "What is it?"

"Does anyone forget the past? Really forget it?"

"Oh, yes," he assured. "Once it's worked through." Then, "It's hopeful that despite everything, you're courageous enough to want something. It's very painful, I know."

And the pain takes over. Can't I help it? I sit under my high-barred window unable to eat or sleep. I pray for strength; I can't find it. My will winces shut. I don't want to be an actress anymore, and I don't want love. I'm boiling again with dreadful memories. And Zohrman, holding the reins, warns, "You're regressing."

And on top of this, Mother phones constantly. She treats me like a lover: I "pushed her" into an unhappy marriage to Charles, and now she has to swallow the blame for deserting me. Is it my fault she can't love him? Why am I responsible for her misery? She needs me; she wants to see me. Not now, I say. How bitterly her insults repeat on me. I tell Dr. Zohrman I told her, "I don't *want* to see you." The little lie slipped off my tongue; I only wanted to say it. He looked disapproving. Would I like to go into the closet?

DECEMBER 2

Today I woke at three o'clock and missed my session. What was my excuse? I told him my medical doctor gave me sleeping pills.

"Why didn't you ask *me* for a prescription?"

"Because I was afraid you'd think I'd take an overdose. You look angry whenever I ask for one."

"I wonder if you don't mistake my concern for anger."

I wonder if he isn't angry over having constantly to feel concerned. "My death would be none of your business," I said.

"It certainly *is* my business if you're not able to sleep because of your great need for love and your inability to express it." No answer. "To have such a need and not be able to bear it," he droned on, "certainly is a conflict. Why can't you express that need to me?"

"Because you don't want to fill it."

"I told you I wouldn't."

"*Want* to, I said. I'd want you to want to."

Again he's not listening!

"When things get this bad, you call me up!" he shouted.

I feel unreal. I want his permission to die.

"When patients feel that way, continue to feel that way, we put them in hospitals."

"I remember as a child wanting a place to scream; now I think if I could just retreat a while somewhere, not have to see anyone . . ."

"They won't let you do that."

"Why not?"

I'm engulfed in sorrow. My most fervent wish is sleep. Zohrman still visits me in my imagination. Last night he carried an umbrella, walked with me in the rain. We saw a bald man kneel before a child, speak softly, and take her hand. Her ears perked up like petals above the frayed velvet collar of her coat. The coat I seemed to remember, also the child's eyes fixed upon the father—beautiful, listening eyes. We passed houses of apple green, pea green, various shades of gray, magenta, and pink. It was like walking through an avenue of pâtisseries.

DECEMBER 3, 1959

I don't know what I'm doing, I don't know why I'm feeling. I don't know why I have to feel at all. Be quiet, I tell myself, quiet.

You'll see Dr. Zohrman later. Dr. Zohrman will make everything right.

"Tell me your feelings about me," he began.

"I'd rather write about them at home."

"No. In a relationship we do things together."

"I can't."

"Try . . . try to put them into words."

"I can't."

"Try. It's hard to want, isn't it?"

"Yes."

"It's hard to relate, isn't it?"

"Yes."

"You can practice on me."

That night imaginary bugs crawl all over my apartment. Screams tear out of me that I can't stop.

Zohrman hospitalized me at Gracie Square.

LEFT: *My father, Henry Hebald,
and I at the gates of Prospect Park,
Brooklyn, New York, 1937.*

BELOW: *My mother, Ethel Hebald
(right), and I (left) at Long Beach,
New York, 1940.*

ABOVE: *An ID snapshot of me at age thirteen in 1947.*

RIGHT: *In 1954, when I was twenty. Photo © 2001 by Roy Schatt.*

On my wedding day, Jersey City, New Jersey, 1960.

Relaxing in Central Park, circa 1956.

ABOVE: *My mother with her third husband, I. Charles Lifland, circa 1962.*

RIGHT: *My sister, Janice, Long Beach, New York, 1940.*

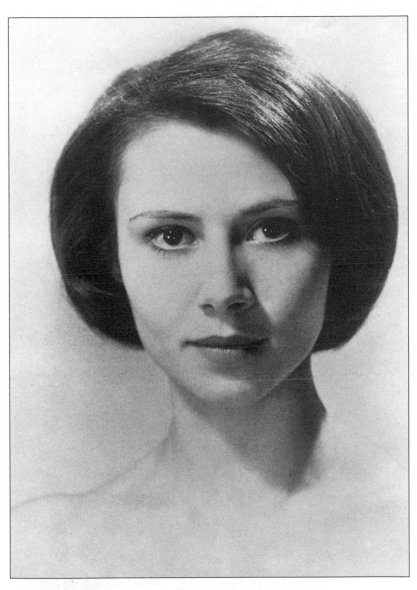

My acting résumé photo, circa 1957, © *by Peter Basch.*

FACING PAGE, TOP: *A scene from Christa Winsloe's* Mädchen in Uniform, *Equity Library Theatre, New York, April 1955. Left to right: Barbara Barrie, me, and Barbara Stanton. Photo © by George Joseph.*

FACING PAGE, BOTTOM: *A scene from Huntington Hartford's adaptation of* Jane Eyre, *Belasco Theatre, New York, 1958. Jan Brooks is on the left.*

ABOVE: *A scene from Tennessee Williams's* The Glass Menagerie, *Crystal Lake Lodge, Chestertown, New York, summer 1959. Alex Cord is on the right. Photo by the director, Walt Witcover.*

RIGHT: *A scene from Yukio Mishima's* Hanjo, *ANTA Matinée Series at Theatre de Lys, New York, November 1960. Ann Hennessey is leaning over me. Photo © by George Joseph.*

BELOW: *My puppy, Gobo, and I in Lawrence, Kansas, 1979.*

PART TWO ～

Chapter Twelve

*T*he top sheet of my first Gracie Square hospitalization record states that Carol Hebald, a white, Jewish actress, twenty-five years old, five feet, five inches, 125 pounds, was admitted to room 528 on December 3, 1959. Diagnosis: paranoid schizophrenic. Further on in this document is a copy of the consent form signed the next day by my mother authorizing my electric convulsive treatments, commonly known as "shock." Mother later told me that when she was refused permission to see me that day, she walked unannounced into Dr. Zohrman's private office and pleaded with him to intercede. When he explained that he had no power to do so, she cried out to him, "Why? What happened?" It was then he told her, "Your daughter went down so fast I had to hospitalize her. Don't you see? She tried to kill herself." I have no memory of this.

≈

I remember my room beetle-green in the morning light, so dank with stagnant air water stood in drops on the walls. Are they sweating for me, I wondered, because I wasn't frightened at all by the frequent wake-up raps at my door: "You have a treatment, Miss Hebald." The word conjured up mud packs, massages, facials—something privileged women got. No, I felt no fear, only intense annoyance at being roused before breakfast to the tantalizing smell of bacon sizzling as I was led in my robe along the corridor for electric convulsive therapy.

"I want breakfast!"

"Later, Miss Hebald."

"Now!"

"You'll choke on it."

"I wouldn't do that!"

"No?"

I remember the plump, dimpled anesthetist who helped me onto the hard table and strapped me safely down. "Just relax," he said, slipping the needle in my arm. With the warmest of smiles, he placed the bit in my mouth to prevent my chewing up my tongue during convulsions. I crossed my eyes in response, at which he shook a finger ("Naughty, naughty") as I floated up-up-up-and-out before the switch was pulled.

Between December 9 and January 8 I received fifteen treatments, supplemented on alternate days by 100-, 150-, and 200-milligram tablets every four hours of the psychotropic tranquilizer Thorazine, the fashionable cure-all known to reduce hallucinations, delusions, and other thought disorders. Although hospital records indicate that on December 11 I was placed on suicide watch, the positive effects of shock must soon after have kicked in, because I remember waking up ravenous at the breakfast table for my rasher of bacon, poached eggs, and coffee. Dr. Zohrman had ordered me a special high-protein, low-fat diet. Sick as I'm told I was, I hadn't forgotten my vanity.

A young, black orderly served me: "Here's your diet, Miss Special."

A short-term facility for most, Gracie Square had frequent turnover. With no occupational or recreational therapy on our fifth, most restricted floor, we met after breakfast in one huge dayroom situated off a long, dimly lit corridor, beyond which lay the locked, slit-windowed doors of our private dormitory-style rooms. Herded together until bedtime, most of us in folding chairs along the dayroom's gigantic, graying walls, we knitted, played cards, watched TV, and learned etiquette from the nurses' aides: "Is that a ladylike way to sit, Miss X, with your legs spread?" I was one among many on suicide watch; some awaited beds at state hospitals, others, at the more elite retreats where several had met before: "Don't I know you from Sheppard Pratt . . . Payne Whitney . . . Menninger's?" Few stayed longer than three or four months.

Among the exceptions was a fireman, a rotund six-footer who, at twenty-three, had been cited for bravery in the performance of his duty. He'd snatched a burning child from a fire and become brain-damaged by the fumes. Joe got such a kick out of being here: "I've already made it, folks!" he'd boast at dinner, piling high his mashed potatoes. He had room, board, and companionship for life. He didn't even have to go out.

And there was Alice, the quietest guest in the house, with an open invitation for life. Heavy, with a wide-cheeked homely face—the image of my good Aunt Fanny—Alice had been here, perfectly silent, for three years. No one urged *her* anymore to relate. She stayed all day in her boxlike room opposite mine and emerged only for meals. Always, she came early and circled the tables like a caged animal eager to eat. She stole the bread; she wasn't ashamed. She'd prowl quietly around, take a slice, jerk it apart, and stuff it into her mouth like cotton. "It's her muzzle," someone snickered. A sympathetic nurse told me, "Alice isn't unhappy. Just don't steer too near, or accidentally touch her—or she'll lunge out at you with her bare hands."

One night the cooks were late with dinner and kept us waiting in the dayroom a solid hour. Locked out of her room, Alice sat alone in front of the communal TV. "May I join you?" I asked, and hearing no answer, angled my chair at her side slightly behind her. There she sat until dinner practicing eye contact with the television news anchor: Each time he smiled, she tried to smile back.

I remember no silver screen schizoids chattering into their beards, no *Snakepit* Hesters, no prostrate Magdalenes. Only occasionally, a woman would dance the two-step, smiling up at an absent partner. There were of course the annoying ones who complained bitterly about having to take medication or submit to treatments. Not I! Dr. Zohrman had clearly explained shock therapy as a temporary measure that represses the intolerable until we're strong enough to confront it. In the meantime, relief. Shock was a blessing, not a punishment! Why did the others make such a fuss about losing their memories? When they found their memories, they lost their minds.

Nor did I balk at first at having my liberty taken away. No telephone privileges, no visitors, no mail? No need to listen or account to others for things I couldn't tell myself.

"You shouldn't be here!" whispered a tall, stately woman to me at dinner. A chronic suicide who'd outlived her welcome at Payne Whitney, "I miss it there—terribly," she confessed. "How can people get acquainted here? Eating at bare card tables pushed against the walls. These cheap paper napkins! There we had a proper dining room with lovely round tables, fresh flowers, linen *serviettes*."

"Switch hotels," sniped a passing orderly.

"And the kindness, the kindness. Not these little . . ."

"Please don't cry."

"What are you doing here?" she insisted.

Opposite was my new Italian roommate, a modest, middle-aged matron, who on her first night kept pleading, "Help me, help me."

"What is it?" I'd asked finally, leaning over her bed.

"Hurt—so bad." She touched her chest, her throat. I took her hand and held it till she quieted.

Just now she was telling her neighbor that she felt so alone when she first came to America, the only reason she didn't commit suicide was that she was afraid they'd print her real age in the newspapers.

Although most of us kept silent about the humiliations that brought us here, I was quick to detect in the few who spoke a slight note of pride that betrayed the subtext: my story is worse than yours, my suffering greater. But I've always been quick to perceive in others faults I'm ashamed of in myself.

I remember the morning a fair, white-coated gentleman joined me at the dayroom window. "Are you waiting for someone?" he asked. I didn't know. Taking my arm he led me to his office: "I'm Dr. Warren." I warmed to him right away. Kindly, soft-spoken Dr. Warren was a visiting resident from London who stayed just a little while. Of our few interviews, only the memory remains of his whole face lighting up with excitement at my passionate outburst, "No one has a right to ignore children!"

I don't know how soon after completing my series of treatments I was allowed visitors. I must have told Freddy where I was, because he was with Mother and Janice the day Dr. Warren said I was doing better and might soon be let out on pass. They were couched in the visitors' enclave, between two orange plastic vases filled with purple and white plastic flowers. "Can we see her now?" asked Mother impatiently.

"Yes," said the receptionist. "One at a time."

Mother, spotting me in the dayroom, sailed brightly across with the announcement, "You're coming home with me next

week! And I'm going to cook you the most wonderful . . ." When
Dr. Warren, at her heels, shouted furiously, "Don't get her hopes
up. For Christ's sake stop fooling her!"

Days, weeks passed. I was with the knitting klatch one afternoon, gabbing as usual about the starchy food and lack of exercise, when my neighbor turned to me and exclaimed, "You were
so sick."

"Why? What did I do?"

"I don't think it's fair to say."

"Oh, come on! You can't tell me that and leave me hanging."

"You talked to yourself all day at the window."

"Is that all?"

We were interrupted by the dark, full-throated screams of a
young German woman locked in isolation just beyond the dayroom wall.

"How can anyone have any peace with Grete here?" she complained.

"She's getting something out of her system. I wish *I* could."

"But she's annoying us! Why don't they put her out of her misery?"

"Here she comes," warned a passing aide. "Watch your purses."

Each day at three o'clock, Grete joined us for half an hour.
Moving gracefully across the dayroom on her short, sturdy legs,
her light brown hair flowing, Grete from afar resembled a child
dancer. Only the great gray wells of her eyes and the ashen tone
of her skin revealed a woman of perhaps twenty-eight. How long
since she'd seen daylight? I didn't ask. Waving her cigarette for
friendly Nurse Maude to light, Grete pooh-poohed her warning,
"I have my eye on you!"

How *could* she with so many distractions? Like the pitched
cries of passengers on the deck of a sinking ship:

"Nurse, why am I here?"

"Nurse, I want to go home."

"Talk to your doctor."

"I'm talking to you!"

A turn of wind, a quick rush of steps. Someone can't open the door. Everything everywhere locked: "Nurse, I can't get out!"

Meanwhile Grete would be halfway around the room on the lookout for an open purse to drop her lit cigarette in. The day she dropped it in mine, I removed it, took a puff, lit a fresh one from it, and gave it to her. She smiled:

"What's your name?"

Every day we'd seek each other out, and arms entwined, smoke, exchange smiles, significant glances. Occasionally we'd comment on the others. Will we ever forget "Alice in Wonderland," a pert, bluebulb-eyed blonde in plaid, pleated skirt, her slim young thighs advancing on us like a colt's:

"I'm a maniac depressive. What are you?"

All those labels! Schizophrenic, melancholic, suicidal.

"Here comes the lightbug," muttered Grete, watching a bent, balding young man reach for the dayroom light switch to play: off-on-off-on-off-on.

"Doctor, stop that!" hollered the nurse.

"Doctor, stop that!" mimicked Grete.

"He's a doctor?"

"Like my brother."

Grete's brother was a psychologist. Where was he? She didn't know; I didn't press it. We treasured our silences. For years I'd love them back to life again in my thoughts. And our few words. Whatever we said carried weight, not because everything was fraught with meaning, but because we never spoke unnecessarily.

"You don't talk to yourself anymore," she observed one day.

"In public. Because someone pointed it out. It helps me sort my thoughts. Does that make me crazy? It's when I can't listen to others I'm in trouble."

"And when I can't scream." I leaned forward to hear more but she turned away.

"Why do the doctors keep asking us if we have feelings of unreality? What does that mean?" I asked.

"Just a question from some standard theory," she sighed.

"Which one?"

"Who knows? They have theories to make anything inexhaustible."

Wasn't it so? It seemed every theory I'd ever heard on the subject of déjà vu, for example, existed for the sole purpose of denying what my instincts told me: that I *had* been in a particular place before. That didn't mean I had, only that the possibility existed. Why deny it?

"They're scared of the unknown," she said.

෴

"What are *you* doing here?" asked the psychologist of me at dinner.

"Same thing you're doing."

"Wasting time," he grunted.

"No. You'll be a better doctor for this."

"Well, touché!" as though the thought had never entered his mind.

Grete shouted from isolation all next day: "I want some fish, do you understand? Fish! I want some fish." Over and over and over. Finally, at three o'clock, she came over to me, pale as death. We smoked in silence.

"You look depressed," I said finally.

"Just depressed? I'm suffering from past events I can't recall," she joked weakly.

The next day she disappeared. I didn't know where; I didn't know why. It was against hospital policy to tell me. I was never to learn if her screams eventually helped, or sent her so deep into torment, she was unable ever to come out.

The effects of shock had worn off, and my attendant mood drops resumed. I was started on a new regimen of pills: the old standbys Thorazine and Mellaril to calm me, and the mouth-drying antidepressant Tofranil, which kept me awake all night. I'd wander the halls looking for Grete. Warned to stay in bed once, twice, three times, I was put in isolation. I remember a small, square, padded room with no toilet. I asked to go several times. But Grete wasn't there, either.

Shut out from work, from friendship, my mind grew inhibited and my thoughts inaccessible. All around me people were talking. But words failed their meanings; seldom were they connected to their speakers. Was this the effect of pills, or Grete's absence? When it was possible to think straight, I did nothing but consider my confusions:

"'Absence makes the heart grow fonder,' or 'Out of sight, out of mind?'—which is true?" I asked Dr. Zohrman, who came to visit.

"Which is true for you?" he asked.

"You know, it used to help me to write things down. Maybe if I took notes . . ."

"Why don't you do that?" he suggested.

I filled a small scratch pad I kept with me at all times, by day in my purse, at night under my pillow. It was always possible to borrow pencil stubs from the nurse. I returned all but one that I peeled down with my fingernail.

JANUARY 15

Late last night a delicate old woman, who appeared to have lost something, wandered into my room. An aide caught her and demanded she leave. "She's not bothering me," I said. The lady flashed me a grateful smile as the aide led her out. I dozed off, then woke a few minutes later to find her standing over me. Next thing I knew, she was screaming; two orderlies were pulling her along the corridor by her hair.

This morning at breakfast, as though a dam had burst within her, she talked nonstop about her life. "Shut up, can't you?" snarled her neighbor. "You haven't shut your mouth once—not once!—since you sat down."

"Excuse me," she said quietly. "I haven't spoken to anyone in so long."

Nor have I. Tomorrow I'm to be allowed home on a trial pass. I'm told if all goes well, I might be released next week.

FEBRUARY 1

They changed their minds. *Why?* I didn't do anything wrong. I just feel tired, and older. I'm still only twenty-five, but I'm older—as though all my life I was too young to be a failure, and all of a sudden I've come of age.

FEBRUARY 15

Most unusual! Last week I was allowed on a special pass to audition for an Off-Broadway production of Chekhov's *The Seagull.* I'm cast as Masha, and may rehearse on condition that I return immediately afterward to the hospital. I'm happy. Hold it, you jerk! Let the doctors *see* you happy, and then they'll let you out.

FEBRUARY 22

Sunday, home on pass, I got a surprise visit from Dr. Lou Scarrone, Henry's friend from my Sapirstein days. He tried to sleep with me. How did he know I was there? Mother had called him early this morning and told him. He spent an entire hour comforting her. Was it my fault she woke him? Does he think that gives him the right...? I'm so confused. I told him I was due back at the hospital, then after he left, thought again of suicide.

MARCH 5

They released me on February 27. I've been out only a week, and already, I've taken an evening job checking hats at the Roundtable Restaurant. Days I rehearse *The Seagull,* and see Dr. Zohrman twice a week. How gentle he's suddenly become. He sees me fighting an undertow, dragging myself to shore:

"How do you feel?"

"Not too hot."

"Remember, one day at a time. You've been through a harrowing experience."

Harrowing? I don't recall it as such, unless shock burned it out of my mind. That's not all it burned. I love it when actors embrace me on the street—"Dahling, where *have* you been?"—and I don't know who the hell they are. Freddy calls constantly, a faithful friend. I gained ten pounds in the hospital, and still I'm bingeing on starchy soups, spaghetti, ice cream, and cookies. Dr. Zohrman says these binges stem from my insatiable need for love. And I groan. He goes on: They signify my wanting to eat up love objects. But not to worry. There hasn't been a cannibal in New York City for quite a few years.

Our *Seagull* director got a job on the West Coast, and our production has been indefinitely delayed.

MARCH 30

A grinning baldy, straight out of my past, flirted with me at the Roundtable hatcheck counter. I told him to get lost. He persisted. "Get away from me!" I screamed.

The manager came over. "What's going on here?"

"*You* figure it out!" I told him and walked off the job. My God, how awful it must be not to have the means to do that. What my mother must have endured in the factories and offices of her youth!

APRIL 12

Last night Freddy begged me to stay overnight with him, and when I refused, charged me with resenting him from the moment I walked in the door. He was right. I accepted his dinner invitation to please Zohrman, who's prodding me again to "relate." What an ugly word! I gag on it.

Freddy wants to see me every night and cries like a woman when I refuse: "Who brought you candy in the hospital? Who stood by you?" I've never known anyone with such a capacity to move me to pity and guilt—anyone but Mother, that is.

APRIL 16

Henry Uffner called and will call again next week. "We'll have lunch," he said. Whether we're going out or I'm supposed to make it I don't know. Oh yes I do! He wants to play around again, but I'm not up to it. Nor do I trust myself to say no. It's safer to disconnect the phone. How ready they are—Lou and Henry both— to send me back to the hospital. They really, really, really, really don't care about me, and I still don't believe it.

APRIL 20

Today Dr. Zohrman admitted that he pushed me too far in therapy and that's why, or part of why, he had to hospitalize me. He's
sincere, dedicated. I never doubted it.

"What was my diagnosis, by the way? Does it have a name?"

"Transference neurosis," he answered, reminding me of how,
reenacting my infancy in his office, I cast him in the exclusive
roles of my parents: "You lost sight of our professional relationship."

I learned only later, from my Gracie Square hospitalization
records, Zohrman's consistent diagnosis of me as "paranoid schizophrenic (prognosis poor)."*

MAY 15

He's been getting tougher: "You've had no more traumas than
anyone else. The only reason you don't function as well is because
you haven't learned to repress as well."

"But you keep telling me how 'extraordinarily deprived' I've
been. Doesn't that contradict . . . ? I don't understand."

"Because you don't understand, or because it doesn't make
you a special case?" A low blow; he saw it and sighed: "Look, all I
meant is you don't have thoughts or fantasies that most people
haven't had at one time or other."

---

*The diagnosis transference neurosis appears nowhere on my Gracie
Square hospitalization records. Dr. Zohrman's diagnosis of me as "paranoid
schizophrenic (prognosis poor)" remained consistent throughout this and
my two subsequent Gracie Square hospitalizations. Since the last two of
these hospitalizations occurred as a result of suicide attempts, and in rela-
tively quick succession, I have for the sake of economy merged them into
one episode in chapter 14.

Then why the hell didn't he say so? Though that isn't exactly true either. I feel him retreating from the front, watching his every step. He wants to be tough, but not too tough. He's afraid I'll break. But chipping away at my defenses is his job, and by God he's going to do it. And I? I know I must go inch by inch with the truth if I hope to be made right again.

MAY 18

"Maybe I can't repress those early traumas because no one let me scream like Grete."

"Who's stopping you?"

"I am," I conceded. "But if I could, if I did . . ."

"If you did?"

"I'm afraid I'd never come back."

"Oh, you'd always come back," he said.

"How do you know?"

"A certain ego strength."

MAY 20

Last night Freddy proposed marriage to me. I don't know what to say. Feeling about him the way I do, it wouldn't be right.

Zohrman doesn't agree: "You don't have to be in love to get married, but you do have to want to get married."

"Mother and Jan are certainly pushing it. They tell me marriage will change my life: I'll develop new interests, broaden my outlook."

"What about forgetting the past?"

"By keeping busy at home?"

"Well?"

"I think it would be unfair to Freddy. And if you say one word about my superego . . . "

He laughed merrily. But this was no joke.

"You don't have to *stay* married, you know."

"What? It would break Freddy's heart if . . . "

"I'm here for *you*." I cringed slightly. "And for you to be alone just now is, well . . . " He wanted to say dangerous: "Not good."

"Not good," I echoed.

It crosses my mind but skips my tongue that he's protecting me and, not incidentally, himself. I could say he wore me down, he and Mother both, if there were a "me" to wear. But what about Freddy? What did Dr. Zohrman tell me about treating men like objects? Something is wrong here—terribly wrong. I don't know it yet, but my respect for him has begun to erode.

Nevertheless, at my mother and stepfather's Jersey City apartment, I married Freddy on June 5, 1960. On the morning of the wedding, as I was dressing in her bedroom, Mother stormed in with several friends and, catching me in a bra, cried, "Look, girls! Look what he's getting!"

"How old are you?" one asked me warmly.

"She'll be twenty-six next month," said Mother proudly. Then, "Congratulations, my little old maid!" and shut the door.

Chapter Thirteen

*H*eaded home from our brief Montreal honeymoon, Freddy pulled up to a roadside grocer, who stood watch on his porch. We'd been on the Ruth West Cottage Cheese diet—twenty-four ounces a day. I bought our noon allotment, two eight-ounce containers and some water, and headed back out. There was Freddy's car, but where was Freddy? I alerted the grocer, who waited with me outside. Across the way was a gas station.

"There's your father—over there!" he shouted, spotting Freddy coming out of the men's room. Freddy felt mortified and blamed me later for dressing like a kid. All right, all right. I snapped the rubber band from my ponytail and shook out my hair.

"Put it up," he said. I did so in the car, a perfect little girl.

At first I was moved by Freddy's tenderness and did all I could to deserve it. In our little, rent-controlled apartment on East Sixteenth Street, I made my twenty-five-dollar allowance cover our weekly expenses. He bought me a special, grooved hammer to pound out tough cuts of meat, showed me how to wash and iron his shirts. Although our lovely old building was mouse infested, he wouldn't pay for an exterminator; mousetraps would do just fine.

~

It's fall. At 3:30 Freddy's home from his exhausting job teaching biology at a school for disturbed adolescents. After his snack he unwinds at the desk in the foyer with the *New York Times,* which is delivered every morning. He's remarked more than once that I haven't opened it. Ashamed to admit I still can't read a paper I say, "I just fold it neatly back for you."

"Oh, come on!"

Three months into our marriage, he asks why I don't get a job. Because I'm making acting rounds. Didn't we agree I could? But all his friends' wives worked before they had kids. Whenever he calls his sister, Dotty, at his Farmingdale family home, he waves me from the room. Once I heard him say, "Handle it? How do I handle it?"

~

On November 15 I opened as the lead in Yukio Mishima's *Hanjo* at the American National Theatre Academy's Matinée Series at Theatre de Lys. No sooner had Louis Calta of the *Times* praised my "winning" performance next morning as the insane girl who gives her whole life to waiting, than Uta invited me back as her scholarship student, and suggested me for the role of Gregor Samsa's sister in Anna Sokolow's dance production of Kafka's *Metamorphosis*. It was a great success.

After we closed, Freddy pressed me again to get a typing job to help pay the bills. What bills, I wondered, since our expenses are small and his salary exceeds them. "And why now, when my career is starting to pick up again?"

"Your career? I have more talent in my little finger than you . . . " I walked away. "If I had your advantages," he shouted, "I could have been one of the greatest musicians."

"If you could have been, you would have been—if you really wanted it enough."

Is that so? Well I am never to forget that he hails from a working-class family and I know nothing of his hardships: "Dotty and I never had the leisure to get sick. We worked sunup to sundown on the farm and practiced the piano winter nights with gloves on."

"I'm sorry. But I didn't get married to give up the theater after being on Broadway twice!"

"You'd better stop talking about Broadway," he hands back. "It's been a while."

"For God's sake, what's the matter?" I demand.

It's hard for him to admit, but when actors from scene study come to the apartment to rehearse while he's at school . . . well, he's ashamed for what the neighbors might think.

"Well that's different, very different," I concede. "Would you rather we rehearse at *their* homes?"

"Do you really rehearse? Then pay for a rehearsal hall!"

"Stop making rounds to get a job to pay for . . . ? Who *does* that? I don't understand!"

But I understood only too well. I'm to put obstacles in my path to appease him. Whatever he was denied, I'll be denied too. It's astonishing how like my mother he is. From then on I rehearsed at my partners' homes.

For his birthday I bought him six extra-large shirts, which he struggled in vain to button. He'd gained twenty pounds since our honeymoon, and his students called him Fat Freddy. "It's no use—I can't. I used to be able to." The tears rolled down his cheeks. I wiped them away.

I keep quiet now when he picks on me because I think maybe I deserve it. Sometimes he says dreadful things to provoke me and, when I leave the room, shouts, "At least I'm trying!" He talks me to pieces when I want silence, and I'm silent when he needs me to speak. I'm so repelled by his tireless insistence on his feelings, I keep mine shut inside. His jealousy of my outside interests grows more alarming every day. Soon he wants detailed reports on my weekly sessions with Zohrman. But even Mother, who pays the bill, knows better than to drill me on their contents. "I'm not supposed to discuss it."

I picked up Thomas Mann's *Death in Venice*. He grabbed it and tossed it across the room: "Get that shit out of here."

MAY 2, 1961

Today Zohrman asked what magazines Freddy subscribes to, "just to get some idea of the man you married—and love."

I love Freddy? Then how come I don't feel it? What signs have I given? He certainly doesn't find any. In fact, not a week has passed since our marriage that I haven't wished for his death.

"That's nothing more than your fear of it," sighed Zohrman.

Question: Am I screwed up or Zohrman, so screwed down in the belief that nothing is as it seems, he can't see what *is?*

MAY 18

I stood for an hour today in front of the neighborhood butcher. I don't remember the last time I felt so desolate. I didn't want to put the key in the lock, but I had to refrigerate the meat in my hand.

MAY 29

Guess what? I'm pregnant! I'm going to give birth next February. Freddy says, "Now we'll have a little Carol running around." I'm excited, happy, sad, worried—and God knows what else. Why, suddenly, do I long for my childhood, for Barbara and my big sister Jani?

Freddy's mother has begun to knit. And mine is everywhere apparent. She phoned us last night about a four-room apartment to let for $125 a month. When Freddy said, "No, thank you,"

Mother asked, "Why not? You're making a decent living. Don't you want to better yourself?"

"I said, no, thank you," clipped Freddy.

They've become polite but mortal enemies.

JUNE 14

Today after cleaning the house, I tied a small pillow around my stomach, threw a loose dress over it, and walked to my old neighborhood on the Lower East Side. A grocer waved hello as though he knew me! Women bowed their heads, men smiled and made way for me. I enjoyed myself immensely. When I told Freddy, he warned, "Don't do that again."

"Why not?"

"Because it's sick."

JUNE 19

"You can't stand up to Freddy because you're guilty of your father's death," concluded Zohrman today.

"Maybe. But I don't understand what my father has to do with the deprived little boy I married."

"Don't you?"

"I wonder if I'll have to stop acting after the baby comes."

"There are other ways to create than acting."

"Maybe." I answer "Maybe" more often than I realize, and this annoys him. He says he's on more solid ground when I respond to his theories with an emphatic no, by which he always knows I mean yes, and vice versa. Always?

JULY 15

Summer's here again. Freddy's taken a bass-playing job in Tamarack, New York. We live nearby in a little bungalow colony. Across the way are several women whose husbands come up only on weekends. Weeknights, when Freddy's with the band, "the girls" play mah-jongg together. He wonders why I don't join them. I'm taking care of the sweet kitten he got me for my twenty-seventh birthday. Last night a couple of mah-jonggers peered into my window and caught me reading in bed with Flapdoodle in the crook of my arm.

"Hermit," they taunted. "Awww, she likes the kitten."

Freddy came home at 2 A.M., and on hearing my account of the neighbors, went straight to the window and shouted foul abuses at them for fifteen minutes. I'm grateful their husbands were in the city, and grateful also to Freddy, who still manages somehow to adore me. Last night I adored him, too.

AUGUST 10

My water broke. When the doctor told me, "I think you're going to have a mis," I thought he meant "Miss," as in daughter. I miscarried in the local hospital. I was terrified. The fetus's neck was broken. Now I'm writing furiously: poems, death wishes, prayers. I have the impulse again to scream myself free and clear. The only thing lacking is the place.

"You didn't want my child," accused Freddy.

"That's not true!" I slammed the bathroom door, sat down, and started hemorrhaging. We have no phone. Freddy detests luxuries.

"Freddy!" I called out. Again, "Freddy!"

When he saw the blood, he ran down the road to a neighbor: "Call an ambulance! Quick!"

They carried me from the bed to the stretcher, wrapped me warmly, and bound my head. I began laughing uncontrollably. I knew I might die, and I couldn't stop laughing. The doctor who performed the D and C wondered why it hadn't been done immediately, after I miscarried. Didn't my husband want to lay out the money?

Packing for New York City, I pray for success and for a chance at another baby because I want to give joy to Freddy and my mother. What makes me suddenly such a good little girl?

OCTOBER 21

Last Sunday Milton Hebald called me up! He flew in from Rome with his wife, Cecille, to give a one-man show at the Nordness Gallery. I was thrilled. One of his sisters had sent him my *Hanjo* reviews. He hadn't known there was another artist in the family. He invited Freddy and me to dinner that very night at our second cousin Edith's apartment, where he and Cecille were staying.

The moment we met, I kissed them both on the cheek. Cecille was warm and gracious, but Milton drew back. Did I do something wrong? No. He was quick to explain the Hebalds aren't demonstrative: "We're a cold lot," he said, then emended it later to exclude us! Over drinks, when he reminded me that our fathers were competitors, I pounced immediately on the question of why those five brothers didn't open a common jewelry store way back when. How could they let one of their own commit suicide? Couldn't anyone give him a job?

"They took turns trying to feed him," he answered. "But Bernard wouldn't eat."

"Because he felt them competing for the reputation of generosity," I guessed. Milton nodded, then went on to tell me that Bernard wasn't the only strange one. "Some of the Hebald women . . ." He rolled his eyes as he spoke of a cousin who, after her siblings had married, moved into total isolation; and a niece, solitary since the premature death of her husband, who consents to speak only occasionally on the phone.

There was so much we had to tell each other, but Freddy was monopolizing the conversation. Milton and I stole off to a corner, where he related the story of his father, Nathan's, murder before mine moved in with his family. I wanted to hear more about my father, when the women asked after my mother: "Widowed twice?" "How awful." "Oh, that is *really. . .* "

"She's married again," I told them.

"Well, more power to her!"

OCTOBER 30

Milton's exhibit was brilliant: Figures and bas-reliefs illustrating Joyce's *Ulysses*. "Penelope," "Molly Sleeping," and "Molly Seated" are my favorites. But I cringed today when Freddy phoned him to beg a discount on "one of the smaller pieces" and Milton told him to call his representative.

"I embarrass you?" taunted Freddy. "What's Milton to you? Where was *he* when you needed him? But he sees your name in the papers—after how many years?—and decides to get in touch!"

I've been taking a night course in fiction writing at the local high school. In response to my childhood story, the teacher wrote, "Beautiful, dramatic, poignant—and witty too." I came home beaming. But Freddy was hurt: he should have been the first to see it. When I showed it to him, he admitted, "It *is* beautiful. But if you're serious about writing, why don't you study at a college? I'm sure your mother would pick up the tab."

"Why? Can't we afford it?"

Soon after I discovered that our joint bank account, a wedding gift from Mother, was down to almost nothing because he'd been using it to pay off old debts. "But it's ours. Why didn't you tell me?"

"You keep things from me, I keep things from you." Tit for tat. God, why did I marry him?

I decided to send my story to Milton in Rome. Freddy, seeing me address the envelope, didn't mind telling me he was hurt. I wished he did mind; I wished he had the pride.

"Isn't my appreciation enough?"

"Can't I have another opinion?"

"Why don't you wait till you have something to send?"

"I thought you said . . . "

"You're nowhere near the artist Milton is. Who do you think you're competing with?"

"I'm not competing, I'm sharing."

"Who do you think you're kidding?"

Mamma Freddy! This is ground for divorce. I resolved to leave him the next time we fought. I had no need to start up. He'd oblige soon enough. A few days before Christmas, I bought a tongue from the butcher that was too large for the pot. With Freddy standing over me, I tried to squeeze it in whole.

"Are you really dumb enough to think you can get that tongue in that pot? Cut it!" He handed me a knife.

Handing it back, "You cut it," I said, and got my coat.

"Where are you going?"

"Out."

I never saw him again.

DECEMBER 22

At my mother's and stepfather's in Jersey City, I check my answering service for messages. Freddy has called four times. Mother's absolutely delighted I've left him. She's idle at home with Charles, and welcomes the excitement. This morning, while helping her fold the bedsheets, Charles left his corners hanging: "Look at that!" she said. "He doesn't have a woman's touch."

She didn't know what we were laughing about!

The phone rang. My service again: "Call your husband."

As I dialed his number, Mother whispered to me, "You weak piece of shit."

"You want me to ruin him entirely?"

Freddy picked up the phone: "Where are you?" No answer. "Is there someone else?"

"No."

"That makes it worse." He started to cry. "Where are you?" No answer. "Come back."

"I can't."

"Please. If I can't be your husband, let me be your servant." No answer. "Let me come and kiss you good-bye."

"Stop it!" He was frightening me. "Stop it! I've left you—that's all." I hung up. Mother was satisfied.

Ever since my breakdown, so vital is Mother's need to control me, she believes she's pulling the strings. This morning she asked Janice on the phone, "Should I feel guilty for wrecking Carol's marriage? Charles thinks I should." Whenever Charles criticizes her, Mother runs to Jani for support. Pressed into service, Jan obliges. Mother has become the baby in the family. And Charles is as lonely as my father once was.

DECEMBER 24

Zohrman approves wholeheartedly of my move: "When you married Freddy, it was the right thing to do; now to leave him is the right thing to do."

"If I were in his shoes, I wouldn't think so."

"Are you living for him or yourself? He treated you badly, remember?"

"And I him."

"You're overreacting. Your guilt has nothing whatever to do with the pain you're causing him, and everything to do with your anger."

"I don't know what you're talking about."

"You look on Freddy as a parent," he explained. "One isn't supposed to hurt one's parents; hence, your guilt." I sighed deeply. "Where did you get such a big superego?" he boomed for the umpteenth time. Can't he just say "conscience"? I don't know why he has to fasten my every response to the past. Can't I be guilty for leaving Freddy because I was wrong to marry him in the first place? Zohrman may have urged it, but I took the vow.

I'm working nights at an insurance company and have moved to an Upper West Side studio, where yesterday I got a wonderful letter from Milton. He loved my poems and story. "Can we hope for more of them?" he asked. I'm incredibly dear to myself. For a while.

~

How ripe and ready I am, after my Mexican divorce, to fall for my lawyer, Herbert Popkin. Jan's former boss, he considers himself "a friend of the family." He lives in Westchester with his wife and children, and wants to visit me at home. But he's a busy man. Once a week is all he can manage. I live for his phone calls, which come always at the last minute. "Want to?" he asks, managing never to give his name. He won't chance taking me out, even for a cup of coffee. How tell him without having to say it: Bring me *just once* something besides sex. Zohrman gave me the words; I taped them to the phone, and next time Herbert called, rattled

off casually, "Oh, by the way, would you mind picking up a bottle of scotch on your way over?"

He brought a cheap, undrinkable brand. I took a sip. "Shall I
pay you back?" I asked.

His slack-seamed jowls tightened: "What do you take me for?"

Ten minutes later, he wanted to read my diary to see what I
wrote about him. No, that's my property. Then, "Did you tell Dr.
Zohrman about me? Does he know my last name?" How could I
not know how profoundly I detested this man?

When he called Zohrman to ask whether, as my attorney, he
should advise me to go back to the hospital, I got so upset, Zohrman increased my Thorazine. Later that week I saw an acting
classmate give a brilliant performance on television and came
close to throwing myself off the roof. Everyone's succeeding but
me. The doctor would feel "less concerned" about me in a hospital. Sorry, I said. I'm up for the lead in an Off-Broadway show.

I got it! It's a dreadful play called *The Love of Two Hours.* We're
all hoping for personal reviews. During the rehearsal period, I
offered to buy Herbert a ticket. "Can I bring my wife?" he asked.
I had no will, no power to resist.

Opening night I was off, way off. Technique alone got me
through. No sooner had the curtain rung down than Milton and
Cecille rushed backstage.

"I thought you were in Rome!"

"We're flying back in the morning. We came to negotiate another show. You should have written us about this."

An awkward pause. "I noticed you smiled a great deal," observed Milton.

Then Herbert was shaking my hand. "You did yourself proud."

"I thought you were adorable," said his wife.

Early Saturday morning Herbert showed up at my door with

the morning papers. Although the play was massacred, my re-views were generally good: "Carol Hebald gives a professionally superior performance as the rather silly heroine," wrote the trade paper *Backstage*. The *Journal American* reviewer was vicious to the play and everyone in it, including me: "Carol Hebald smiles a great deal, even when she is supposed to be unhappy."

"Stop feeling sorry for yourself," chided Herbert, browsing through the papers. "There are other things happening in the world." I made no answer. After breakfast he took me to bed: "You're such a good fuck."

"Isn't there anything else?"

The show closed that night. I came home, took an overdose of sleeping pills, and phoned the Hebalds in Rome.

"I called to say good-bye." Cecille kept me on the phone long enough to find out where I was. Milton called our cousin Edith, who hired a police escort to rush me to the nearest hospital to have my stomach pumped.

On November 2, 1962, I was back at Gracie Square.

Chapter Fourteen

*F*irst the stout, berry-eyed admissions doctor: "'People in glass houses shouldn't throw stones,'" he quoted.

"Vulnerable people shouldn't attack others?" He checkmarked his clipboard. "But why someone would move into a glass house where anyone and everyone could look in—?"

"Oh, wouldn't you like that?" he asked, with a sharp, inquisitive smile.

"I? Depends who was watching."

He threw his head back and laughed. "Sooooh . . . 'A rolling stone gathers no moss.'"

"You know, I've been wondering about that for a long time."

"Well, wonder about it now . . ."

"*You* here again?" asked friendly Nurse Maude, Grete's old gatekeeper, who lit my first cigarette:

"Is she around?" No, but the laughing fireman still was; and silent Alice, who, it was rumored, had been given a hysterectomy because she longed so desperately for a child her doctor thought removing the possibility would ease it. Someone heard her say, "Now I'll never have a baby."

Alice talked? Next evening I stood in back of her on the dinner queue. "Hello, Alice," I said. "Remember me?" I put a hand on her shoulder, then instantly withdrew it. Taking her tray to a corner table, Alice, like a walrus, slapped her buttocks down to eat. In her large, kind flesh, her thick flesh, Alice was eating. She tried several times to look up, but neither discerned nor considered what she saw. One object put another out of sight. She was busy eating. She took another bite.

~

• "How beautifully Ruth dances!" sighed Maude, at our Sunday night social. "She's going home tomorrow."

"I know," I said from my seat in the corner. "I'm probably leaving soon too—for Payne Whitney." And tearing open a fresh pack of cigarettes: "I hear the food's better."

"Good luck," she offered quietly. Then, "I'm sorry, Carol."

"Why? They tell me I'm still young."

"You'll get older," she warned, briskly striking a match.

Ruth continued dancing. How lovely she looked, radiant and with child. It seemed a misunderstanding had occurred. Her family had all been "working happily in therapy" with a doctor who, during her private hour, seduced her:

"I went down faster than a one-egg pudding," she told us in her lilting Alabama drawl. "He kept telling me, 'Do you know how attractive you are?' *I* know how attractive I am, despite this excess poundage!"

"But why did you . . . ?"

"Because he said it would help me. But no one here would believe it—not till they found out *he* got sick too. He's resting now at another hospital."

"How awful!" I said.

"They're only human."

"I know, I know. They do terrible work."

"In the name of science, Carol, remember that."

"And are they scientists themselves?"

"They try to be, some."

I drifted off. No doctor, sane or crazy, had ever tried to seduce me. Mine, for the most part, had been dedicated men. They

wouldn't fool with their deeply troubled ones, those they nourished in silent relationships that extended beyond the analytic
hour. Several dancers wandered over to the refreshment table. A
new record blared on the phonograph. My roommate, Elena, a
young Greek woman, came over to me with a bowl of goodies.

"You have wonderful, slim figure," she said, setting it in my lap.
"Eat."

"No, thanks, Elena. Later, maybe."

"Then come and dance," she persisted.

"Please, I don't want to."

She threw up her hands. "How possible? So beautiful . . . Why
not?"

Several hours earlier, her whole family had come to visit: her
muscular, longshoreman husband, three dimpled, fat baby girls,
her brothers, cousins, uncles, aunts. They'd brought her flowers
and hunks of halvah, which she sneaked to me, as I read alone
nearby. For an hour they laughed and ate. Elena, too, seemed to
join in the fun.

"Visiting hours is over!" announced the orderly. And the doors
locked shut. Then it came—the invasion of hell on her spirit that
sank her into a soundless sea, where she lay unable to speak or
move, in which she grew rigidly compelled to stay, and finally,
from which she could not emerge: the waking death of the catatonic stupor.

"Can you understand that?" carped my neighbor. "With all
that love?"

A nurse bustled over to Elena with a shot of Thorazine. Half
an hour later she had recovered, and ate dinner with a hearty appetite.

Maude blew the whistle promptly at ten. Our social had ended. An aide ushered us down to the nurses' station, where we

lined up single file outside her half door for our evening sacra-
ments. I said good-bye to Elena and wished Ruth luck at home.
"And you," returned Ruth solemnly. "Wherever you're going,
have faith. Just chip away at it."

Yes, for me a long-term hospitalization at Payne Whitney had
been indicated. Still, because there'd been some question in Dr.
Zohrman's mind and mine about the wisdom and timeliness of
such a move, I agreed to get a second opinion from his consulting therapist, who came the very next evening.

"You can bring in your coffee," said the aide, summoning me
from dinner. "Just don't spill it on his papers."

I held the cup upright as he glanced over my chart. Large,
round, pink-shaven, his cherubic cheeks reminded me of a child
so adorably regular he makes everyone else feel peculiar. "How
are you doing on the medications?" he piped in treble tones.

"Okay, I guess."

"Thorazine, Mellaril, Tofranil, Tuinal, *and* chloral hydrate—
two barbiturates? *And* thyroid and Dexamil, too?"

"I'm an actress with a too-healthy appetite. I just had some
bad luck in a show. Did Dr. Zohrman tell you?"

"No side effects from the other stuff?" he cut in sharply.

"Just dry mouth, constant thirst." He tapped his pen lightly on
his desk. Was that it? I nodded. But if the pills took the edge off
my anguish they replaced it with an overriding gloom. Everything inside me blunted, I longed for the mood-elevator shock.

Putting aside my chart: "What do think your main problem
with Dr. Zohrman is?" he continued.

I emptied my coffee cup quickly and placed it carefully under
my chair. "I think we've been at a standstill too long. I have to
conquer the shame I feel—over needing."

"Needing?" He frowned.

"Other people. At last night's social, for instance—I guess you know my history? The 'transference neurosis' I was diagnosed with the first time?"

"What about last night's social?" Stick to the point.

"Well, I wanted to dance like the others, but I couldn't. It was more important to spite Dr. Zohrman—who wasn't even there!—by sitting tight, not giving him the satisfaction of helping me."

"Why?" He perched forward.

"Because I imagined him gloating over his success, not being happy for *me* if I danced." Did I need to explain further? I wasn't sure. "I suppose you heard I tried to kill myself to spite him before."

"You *knew* that and yet . . . ?"

"Oh yes I knew!"

I wanted him again to ask why, when he reached quickly across the desk for his papers and, jotting something down, asked what sort of parts I played onstage. Sensitive young women, I replied. At which he rose and snapped shut his briefcase. "I suggest when you leave Payne Whitney, you look for a job as a bitch."

Why didn't I cry out, Wait . . . listen! The fault wasn't mine alone. Hadn't Dr. Zohrman admitted to pushing me too far? Transference neurosis has nothing to do with loving without hope for six years a doctor who urged me to "practice" on him! Why couldn't I say that? Because it was easier to take full blame than to realize what drove me crazy.

Nor could I feel the thrust of his insult until later, only that it was too humiliating to repeat. And it had all happened so quickly. Dr. Consultant was in such a hurry, he hadn't even told me his name. I'd tested the limits of his patience. It was a cold, rainy night in April. He probably had a family to rush home to. He'd put the bitch in the kennel. Now for a bit of relaxation. . . .

A week later Dr. Zohrman came to visit. My bed at Payne Whitney was ready. I'd walk over the next day with my mother. I wasn't to think I hadn't made progress with him. In the beginning I had believed my delusions without question; that wasn't so anymore. I should plan at least a year away, and mustn't expect it to be easy. But from it I might hope to emerge (creep forth?) if not triumphant, then a *real person* with needs that I'd be a better actress for admitting.

"Will you come to visit me?" I asked.

"Once, after you're settled in. You'll have a doctor there."

"And after I leave?"

"Why don't we see how you feel?"

And on this we shook hands.

That night I tossed and turned in my blankets. What were my "delusions"? If I couldn't object to what I didn't recall, still less did I realize that chief among them was my misplaced faith in Dr. Zohrman. How had I made progress if I couldn't control my impulse to spite him—spite *him* for the express purpose of spiting myself—so I could later mourn my fate, and all the while be aware of this?

But then no matter my feelings, I tried to rally my faith: I am not ending up in a hospital. This is only the beginning. It'll be like enrolling at a university for the education of my sentiments. If I could look on treatment as discipline from those stern and loving taskmasters I'd always longed for . . . What, after all, had I longed for? Not compassion alone, but that "intelligent heart"* by which man has been known to resemble the angels. Surely there'd be one among them I could give my mind to, as I'd first given it to Dr. Zohrman, but then somehow had lost. Well I guess

---

*This phrase is Jean-Paul Sartre's.

166

I was just too hard a nut for him to crack. Anyway, he had no choice but to lock me up. I'd been "dangerously depressed, dangerously suicidal" most of my life. In fact, it's a great wonder I wasn't dead.

4 A.M., still I couldn't sleep. I thought I heard someone crying. Someone seemed constantly to be crying. I rose from my bed and looked into Alice's room. She lay, as always, with her knees drawn up and her face covered, fighting an ever-losing battle with longing. Longing so intense that in itself it is madness. Longing of so fierce a nature, it had the power to turn her into a maniac. A lifetime filled with fierce wanting.

~

On the afternoon of April 30, 1963, Mother and I walked the brief eight blocks south from Gracie Square to the Payne Whitney Psychiatric Clinic of New York Hospital. We thought the exercise would do us good. I was carrying a small valise that held, aside from a few toilet articles, a pair of slacks, a blouse, and three simply cut, identical spring dresses in red, blue, and green. I also had with me the complete two-volume set of Proust's *Remembrances of Things Past*, which an intelligent friend had suggested I read.

"Here we are!"

I touched the polished metal address plate of my new home: 525 East Sixty-eighth Street. "The elite psychiatric retreat that houses beggars for love in chic clothing," some Gracie Square regular had mocked. I gazed up at the clean, white-faced structure, its eyelike windows dim and small. Was anyone looking out? I searched for the outpatient clinic, where I had first seen Dr. Fitzpatrick—how many years ago?—as though he might still be on the grounds. Mother called me back. It was time to go in.

An empty lobby, graceful and dark, with green walls and shining mahogany tables—the quiet order and elegance so soothing to the disorganized mind. We were ten minutes early. The receptionist asked us to be seated. A scrawny young "whitecoat" swept hurriedly in the door:

"Hi!" called out Mother. Pointing to me: "She's new!"

"De*light*ed," he replied, with a dash of affectation that smacked of the coxcomb.

"Mother, why are you always so friendly?"

"Because you hate the whole goddamned world," she snarled. "Let's sit down." Fingering the gold nail heads on her armchair: "Look at the *de*tail here!" She ran her hands over the lush green upholstery. We looked at each other and sighed. Eight more minutes.

"I'm going to Acapulco," I declared suddenly.

"I'm going with you," echoed Mother, like a little girl.

"Seriously. Do you think if I left, they'd follow me?" I asked.

"I don't know."

"Neither do I." What ambiguities lay in consenting to one's own commitment? No one had brought me in an ambulance this time. "I guess I'd better stay." Her tears welled up. "Oh, please don't," I said. "If they see you crying, they'll think you're crazy, too." I handed her a Kleenex.

She smiled, then, shaking a playful finger at me, "Remember, I'm not dying until you get married again."

"You may very well be immortal."

The elevator doors opened promptly at two o'clock. A nurse—sturdy, large-boned, professionally cheerful—stepped toward us: "Miss Hebald? I'm Nurse O'Brien. Follow me, please." I rose.

"Yoo-hoo! Can I come too? I'm Carol's mother." Again, a pleasant little girl.

"Yes, but only for a few minutes."

Heads bowed, we rode to the seventh floor. An immaculate,

sea-green carpet; diagonally opposite, a spacious room with three neatly made beds. "Yours will be the center one, Miss Hebald."

"But will she get enough air?" asked mother anxiously.

"Oh, yes. And she'll have her daily walks in the garden."

"What about the closet space?"

"Mother, I brought three dresses!"

"Are you forgetting your slacks?"

"There are no slacks at Payne Whitney," advised Nurse O'Brien. "Dresses and skirts and blouses only."

"Just a minute, now." Mother, slightly confused, walked over to the closet and tried the locked door. "This is stuck," she said. "It'll have to be fixed."

"Perhaps you'd like to see the lounges," suggested the nurse.

"Where *is* everyone?" queried Mother, peering into the ample bedrooms spaced comfortably apart along the corridor.

"They're sunning themselves on the roof."

I stopped to observe a painting. "How many patients on this floor?" Mother asked

"Last count was fifteen."

"And in the whole stable?"

"Maybe eighty-five or six. They work their way down and out." Seven floors: the seven *peccata* of purgatory.

"Are there any young men here?" Down to business now.

"She means male patients," I explained.

"Of course, ma'am. This is Seven South; the men live across on Seven North. They get together for daily activities and meals."

"Where they're encouraged, I suppose, to carry on conversations?"

"Mother, please!"

"Mother, please nothing!"

"Mrs. Hebald . . . "

"Mrs. Lifland," corrected Mother regally.

"Mrs. Lifland," parroted Nurse O'Brien, swiftly reversing direction, "I'm afraid it's time to go."

"Oh." Mother stood suspended, an errant child dismissed. Nurse O'Brien led her to the elevator.

"Good-bye, Mommy," she said, quickly pecking my cheek. "See you soon." Another tear, a quick intake of breath. Then, "What's for dinner tonight?"

"Roast beef."

"She'll enjoy that. She likes it rare."

The elevator arrived to take my mother away. In three months I'd be thirty.

~

Enough! I've had enough! In the midst of the blizzard of '96, I've had to come up again for air, and I don't want to go back. What's wrong? I don't know where to begin. Yesterday I phoned the Payne Whitney medical records consultant, whom I'd written months ago for my hospital records. She can't document my stay. "Are you sure you were here?" she asked. "Eleven months: April 30, 1963, to April 1, 1964!" Is that what's disturbing me? That as a former inpatient, my word is so easily doubted? No, I can't go back yet. A bitterness is riding over me, palpable and hard, at the notion of serving myself up on a platter, again to be picked apart. I can't toss Dr. Consultant out of my mind. Sometimes I imagine I've been tortured into sanity by doctors who believe that anyone blessed with my advantages has no business being sick. Is that a paranoiac thought? To see plots and counterplots where none are supposed to exist is not exclusive to the sick. The sick make known their fears, the rest of us keep silent: we put the sick away, we put our fears away.

I hear a shout from my memory: "Say it outright, doctor! My

behavior's inappropriate. Don't play with me like a cat with a mouse. It's barely civil."

"You're behaving inappropriately."

It's possible for me to go on only because the end is in view. What I know now I couldn't even guess at then. My mind was as far from my tongue as my thoughts from my feelings. How to render death in life? If I could paint it without words.

⁓

After my shower and routine breast exam—I was promised a full physical the next day—I was ushered back to Seven. My clothes hung up, my closet locked, I strolled along the corridors. The place was solid, light, and clean as a well-scrubbed convent. Conventual also in attitude was the sober, white-capped staff.

A few minutes later, the evening nurse, homely and kind, peered into my room with a smile: "I'm Nurse Hanni. We've had a squint at your things. There's stuff that's taboo. We took your cigarettes—both cartons."

"Why can't I have—?"

"You can't have them all. You're allowed a pack a day. We'll dole them out to you. Floor rules are posted on the back of your door. No, keep it open, please. Just come into one of the lounges when you're finished."

I ran down the schedule quickly. Every morning at six o'clock our blood is drawn and temperatures taken. At 6:30 we rise and dress. Our beds are made for us. All meals are served and supervised by registered nurses. After breakfast, weather permitting, we're taken to the rear garden downstairs, where we march around in pairs until chimes ring for occupational therapy (O.T.), recreational therapy (R.T.), then lunch. An hour of bed rest follows.

At two we repeat O.T. and R.T., after which (weather permitting) we ascend for half an hour to the small, high-gated roof. Downstairs we play board games or cards until dinner. More group activities until nourishment. Then evening medications, baths, and bed. So ends our day at this time-honored teaching hospital, which changes in my mind as I write this from a convent to a cross between Menninger's and the Quantico Marine Base.

We're not excused from meals until the flatware has been counted twice. Our cue to rise is "*Silvercheck!*" If a piece is found missing we must strip. Each time we use the toilet, a nurse waits outside the unbreakable, glass-partitioned door.

We're summoned thrice-weekly from activities for thirty-minute interviews with our therapists where behind the closed doors of our private and semiprivate rooms, our anger may sometimes be provoked for the purpose of "healthy self-assertion." However, since we're here to regulate, not release, our feelings, shouting is forbidden at all times. We may not slam doors. Nor, indeed, may we open them. All are locked: bureaus, closets, and bathrooms.

Because of our heavy doses of chlorpromazine (the generic name for Thorazine), few of us lose control. I drink several glasses a day of this chalky white substance and think I'll draft a novel called *Concrete in Christ*. Speaking of Whom . . . I learned on the very first night that although a sensible belief in God is encouraged, one must be careful not to be caught in too fervent a prayer.

Last week, before I arrived, a fire had swept through our clinic laundryman's Harlem tenement, killing all four of his children. He was admitted on Seven North. It was rumored that at three this morning, he'd broken out into passionate prayer, when the night nurse rushed to his side with the reprimand: "Mr. Munos, you're disturbing the others." In her hand was a hypodermic needle.

Chapter Fifteen

*I*n midafternoon of my first full day at Payne Whitney, I entered a carpeted, three-cornered alcove, one of several small lounges on elegant Seven South.

"What *were* you?" asked a gentleman in a wing chair with an old issue of *Time* in his lap.

"Have I really arrived in the land of shades?"

"I'm afraid so. I'm Arthur—excused today from activities. A bad cold. They're letting me wander through. Sit over there." He pointed to the lady's chair opposite. "Your first time here?" he asked, loosening the hook on a plaid silk kerchief tucked around his neck.

"Yes. I just came from an all-day physical."

"Met your therapist yet?"

"No; only my roommates, Bernice and Iris."

"The free patients." He scanned me quickly; then, with the air of someone who knows his place in the hierarchy well enough to assume mine: "They have to take *some*. It's a teaching hospital. They learn from us, you know." He paused for a response. "What *were* you?" he repeated.

"An actress."

"Oh? And what did you do?"

"To get in here you mean? Took an overdose of pills."

"Tried to slit my throat," he rejoined, and quickly shut his magazine. I met his watery, brown eyes, deep pockets sunk into his cheeks: an old young man.

"Arthur, do you think we're competing?" I asked.

"For what?"

"For who's sicker."

"What do you think, we're crazy or something?" He readjusted his kerchief. "This hook is killing me; they won't trust me with a flat pin. Can you believe it?" I wagged my head. "Last month I published a novel. Sales, reviews, hails. What am I doing here?"

"Arthur, what's the matter?"

"I don't know from what to die."

I smiled. "Did you just make that up?"

"Make what up? Listen, I'm passing the book around, case you want to get on the list."

"Thanks. I'd love to."

At four o'clock the elevator doors opened. "The stragglers from the roof," he announced. "That's Philipa. Hi, Phipsy!" He saluted a small, muscular woman of fifty who, from the rear, looked seventeen. "The tall one trailing her is Flossy. They're always fighting. The inseparable delinquents from the Social Register."

"No kidding!"

"Floor meeting in five minutes!" chimed a pretty young candy striper. "Assemble in the dining room, please."

"Who'll steer our famous author back to his room?" called Nurse Hanni.

"Am I supposed to take umbrage at that?" asked Arthur.

"It's up to you."

We waited at the bare, round tables. I sat with young Iris, whose huge eyes didn't leave me until Bernice-from-Brooklyn (the way she introduced herself) joined us. I liked her fleshy little face. At the next table was Edith Fine, a plump, round-faced widow from Boston, who nodded sweetly and folded her hands.

In wandered Flossy and Phipsy. I caught the eye of a lanky, young sophisticate "attitudinizing" with a cigarillo: "Stephanie. Got a light?" "Carol. Wish I had." A fair, pasty-faced gentleman in his thirties took a seat at my table. Nurse O'Brien followed in with two aides.

When Dr. Eggertson entered briskly and clapped hands for attention: "Good afternoon! We'll start with a quick review for the new arrival, Miss . . . " He inspected his chart: "Herbald, where are you?" "*Hee*bald." I raised my hand. He introduced himself, then went on to explain that floor meetings at Payne Whitney differed from ordinary group therapy in that we'd talk only about the here and now. "You're invited to air grievances about the staff, one another—even me!" And inclining his large head to a slight twitter of laughter, raised it sharply: "Questions? . . . None? Who'll begin?" he barked brightly. "One at a time."

He took a seat near the door. He crossed his legs. He crossed them the opposite way. He hung his head in silence. The pasty-faced gentleman raised his hand. "Yes, Dr. Peterson?"

"Yes . . . well, I don't mind saying I don't like being asked publicly right after dinner whether I've moved my bowels. Can't they wait half an hour? At Menninger's it's asked in private."

"Comments?" A murmur of ascent, several nods. "Duly noted."

"When were you at Menninger's?" I asked.

"You don't need to answer that," intercepted Eggertson.

"I don't mind," rejoined the other. "I'm a psychiatrist there on leave, a patient here."

"Thank you," I mumbled awkwardly. "I'm sorry if . . . "

"Other questions?" Eggertson's keen-glancing eyes were on me.

"No. Yes. When we present our problems, do we have to identify . . . ?"

"We don't present, we air," he cut in coolly.

"Air?"

"Actors present performances, we air situations. You look confused."

"I am."

He buffed his palms. "Example: Two roommates share a common bath. One complains that the other never washes out her ring. When we discover she'd been suffering for weeks before she confronted the culprit—not in a sensible tone, mind you, but with an ugly insult—we ask her why she waited so long."

"I see. So she's obliged to face up to her own . . . "

"Inappropriate behavior. Exactly."

"The culprit," smirked Stephanie.

"Yes, indeed, Miss Boyle. Our motto is airing and sharing, not . . . ?" he looked briefly around.

"Screaming and swearing," obliged Mrs. Fine.

"Exactly."

"Nice-minded Edith," sniped Stephanie.

Eggertson's eyes brushed past her to the inseparable delinquents, heads bent in whispered battle. "Ladies? Won't you share?"

" 'Scuse us, doctor," said Flossy. "But the other night, when Mr. Munos was caught praying . . . "

"Caught?" cried Phipsy. "Is there something the matter with praying?"

"No!" Flossy smiled, catching Eggertson's eye.

"Indeed not," he agreed. "There's nothing wrong with believing in God."

"Just not too loudly before dawn," chipped in Flossy.

"Exactly." A pause. A polysyllabic sigh. Phipsy was struggling with a thought. "Problem, Mrs. Potter?"

"It doesn't make sense," admitted Phipsy, finally, "to expect us to express inappropriate feelings in a sensible tone of voice."

"His feelings weren't inappropriate," commented Dr. Peterson.

"Right on," from Eggertson. "Point is, he woke up the floor."

"He couldn't help it!"

"He has to *learn* to help it," pursued Eggertson. "After all, why are we here?"

"Why, doctor?" I asked.

"You're here to develop your social skills."

It happened suddenly: Iris threw her chair at Dr. Eggertson's head. Shielding it with both arms, he dashed out the door.

Mrs. Fine was stunned: "Iris, you should be ashamed! In a high-class place like this!"

Iris stood rooted to the spot. I threw my arm around her shoulder, awkward as a bear. Nurse O'Brien stepped between us. "You're not expected to touch," she said in clipped tones.

I walked quickly to my room and opened Proust. Eyes glued to the page, I pretended to read the words, counting the letters and spaces between them. The pretty candy striper peeped in. "What'cha doin'?" she chirped.

"How does it appear to you?"

I couldn't have said what enraged me any better than Phipsy or Iris. But was this a time to teach Mr. Munos social skills? And why assume he lacked them? Because he worked in the laundry room?

A short while later, Nurse O'Brien came by: "Miss Hebald, would you mind joining the others in the lounge? We're having trouble observing you."

"I'm terribly sorry; I'm reading now." She noted something in her chart. "Do you grade us on behavior every day?" I tossed out casually.

"Yes—with comments on attitude *and* effort. Everyone gets individual attention here."

177

"I see. Will you shut the door, please?"

"Doors remain open on Seven at all times."

I looked for Iris at dinner and later, during nine o'clock nourishment. At bedtime I asked Bernice where she was.

"On C.O.–Close Observation. She's really a good kid. We just, like, love to hang out. Except she acts up too much. Take it from me: it's better not to make a fuss, treat yourself crummy."

A nurse threw open our half-closed door and flashed a light, first in Bernice's eyes, then in mine:

"What's the matter?" I asked, alarmed.

"Nothing." She walked out.

"You didn't notice," whispered Bernice. "You were dead to the world last night, but they shine a flashlight in our eyes every fifteen minutes until morning. *And* they censor all our letters."

"Oh, really? Well, they won't censor mine."

"Why not?"

"I won't write any."

"Don't be like that." Bernice yawned.

"How long have you been here?" I asked.

"Seven months; since my son was born. A long time for a postpartum."

"They must be learning from you."

"Think so? You married?"

"No."

She yawned again and curled into her pillow. "Next time my husband visits, you can sneak out your letters with him."

"Thank you!"

Within a matter of days, I mailed my short story to Uta.

The next morning, I was summoned from the garden for my first interview with my British therapist, Dr. Stinta. Wraithlike, crippled, he half rose from a wooden chair and, tossing his clipboard onto my bed, greeted me with a friendly smile. He'd stay only a few minutes today. How was I getting on? Fine. Well, not quite. My eyes traveled to his clipboard. Had my demerit been entered yet? I confessed what happened yesterday and dared to ask after Iris. But curiosity about our peers is not encouraged here. As for rules forbidding touching, "Well they *do* exist for a reason."

"But you don't frown on reading, I hope?"

"You may bring your book into the lounges." The sun spilled in from the window as he rose and extended his hand: a firm grip, a clean, Catholic face, eyes sharp and clear as sapphires. "By the way, do you play bridge?" he asked at the door.

"No."

"It might be a good idea to learn."

He swung it open. Flossy passed by. He greeted her warmly.

Another free patient arrived. Obese, middle-aged, Louise smelled bad because she had nobody to wash for. Everyone avoided her but me. I hated the rough way the practical nurses taught her to bathe: "Here! This way—use soap in there!" Within three days she was gone. So too was Mr. Munos. No one asked where.

The nurses keep bustling to and fro with our trays of liquid chlorpromazine, served in little white paper cups. I gather from our scintillating dinner conversations about its side effects— parched mouths, itching from exposure to the sun—that almost everyone is on it. But we're expected to stay out of the sun. That's why they plant trees in the garden. Most of us emerge into glimpses of our old selves at bedtime, a little drunk on barbiturates, a little stupid. Even those of us who've been silent all day smile in our baths in anticipation of the night. How well we sleep!

"After all this is over, will you come to Brooklyn to see my baby?" Bernice asked me.

"Thanks, I'd love to."

"Don't tell anyone. We're not supposed to keep in touch."

"Why not?"

"I don't know."

It's the stigma, stupid! They don't want us to band together. Get militant about our illness, and people will think we're crazy. I've been here only a few weeks, and already I've learned the unspoken credo of the certified: This above all—to our own selves be true, and it must follow as the night the day, we must be false to everyone. That's why Flossy's so admired. Why she'll graduate with honors—a suicide from the Social Register, who's canceled engagements for years with excuses of skiing weekends in Switzerland that drift sometimes into months "elsewhere on the Continent," when all the time she's been right here.

Phipsy, who's been back three times, and dumb enough to have blabbed, admits to envying wheelchair victims: "At least they're pitied. Us? Not only are we sick, it's our fault for being this way. Of course, no one says it to your face."

"Of course!" snapped Flossy.

～

Today Dr. Stinta asked if I suffer much from jealousy. "Yes," I admitted, "of friends succeeding in the theater while I'm sitting here." But that doesn't excuse my not making use of my time. He's displeased—very, because I still insist on trying to read. "You're missing out on some valuable *experiences*" (emphasis on the *ex*; his diction's so precise he bites me in two with his words).

"But I'm with the others all day in activities. And I relate to Bernice and Nurse Hanni."

"Because they're no competition for you?"

At a stroke he insults us all. I feel Nurse Hanni's dedication, Bernice's warmth. They care; he doesn't. That much is clear. Why, whenever we have an unpleasant exchange, do I pretend an instant later it didn't occur, that some presence between us forbade it?

I got a long letter from Uta. She was fascinated by my story and urged me to continue it from a subjective point of view, then go back and rework it. Nurse O'Brien, who caught me smiling in my bed next morning, thought it very strange. "What evokes this sudden joy?" she asked, pulling up my window blinds. I showed her the letter. She said my response was inappropriate.

"How can a response be inappropriate to a situation she knows nothing about?" I complained later to Dr. Stinta.

"How did Miss O'Brien make you feel?"

"Oh, please! Isn't it clear from the circumstance?"

"You're here to *express* your feelings."

Days pass into weeks. There's a cloud on them now; I can't find them. A cloud. A granite cloud. Granite is my mind. At first I couldn't think; I was good only to feel. Now I can't feel anymore. There's no biological basis for my illness. Why am I on so much chlorpromazine? It clogs me up inside. Smother me, then ask how I feel.

~

Dr. Zohrman came finally to visit. "You're in good hands," he said. I recall nothing else—only his pale, puffy face before me, his deep-set eyes, smaller and sadder than I had remembered them.

Mother came up just after: "So what do they *give* you for sixty-three dollars a day?" she asked pleasantly.

"Lots," I replied, with forced cheer. "Last night, lamb chops, pineapple upside-down cake"—she nodded approval—"heavy cream. I'm afraid I've gained some weight."

"You needed it," she again reassured. "Oh, by the way, I bumped into Dr. Zohrman in the lobby. Has he been up?"

"A little while ago."

"*He* got fat, don't you think? 'Dr. Zohrman, you got fat,' I said."

"You didn't! But when did you see him before?"

"While you were at Gracie Square. Didn't I tell you? He asked my opinion about your coming here. 'No ifs, ands, or buts,' I told him. 'I want that child in a hospital.'" I walked quickly out of the room.

"Carol . . . ?"

Nurse Hanni was in the hall. "Please. My mother . . . please. Tell her I have a stomachache—anything."

"Wait there." When she returned: "Miss Hebald, would you like to shorten your mom's visits?"

"Can I?"

"Certainly. We'll say it's at your doctor's request. What do you want? Fifteen minutes? Less? Five?"

"She comes in from New Jersey. Make it ten."

"No problem. You'll discuss it with Dr. Stinta?"

"Of course. Thank you!"

"Oh, by the way. You're being moved down to Six tomorrow."

~

A blood-red carpet! A private room with a view of the garden; open closets and bureaus. An open bathroom, too. I even get to make my bed.

Three weeks have passed. With fewer activities, I sit for long hours in my armchair sounding out thoughts in my mind. They're my only companions now. I have so many yet few seem to connect. But one keeps recurring in rhythm: "Fresh hot tea in a clean white cup."* I write it down. I write it again.

---

*This became the first line of my novella *Asylum*, excerpts of which were published in *North American Review* (Summer 1970), 35–41.

When feelings become intolerable, I pay attention to the things that bore me—the first lesson I ever learned. I make appointments to remember the dull gleam of an old polished doorknob, a pattern of pimples on a knotty wall, one fat enough to hang a watch on—if I had a watch to hang. I forget how long I've been here. I see the outer shell of everything and everyone. In the garden leaves are falling, sunburnt yellows, reds, and browns. Labor Day has passed. It's been warm a very long time. "We're having Indian summer in October," someone said at lunch.

Today I asked Dr. Stinta if I'm making progress. "Intellectual progress," he said, "but you still tend to speak about your *experiences* without feeling."

Same old problem: how to get off my chest what's not yet on my chest? "Maybe I'm on too much medication," I suggested. He didn't deign to answer. No one can will feelings into being. If actors know that, why don't doctors? I studied his socks, one navy, one black, under the inlaid heel of his shoe. Shifting in his chair, he showed me his light, thin-boned profile: "Why can't you simply say, 'I feel miserable?'" he asked. Because I can't. His very presence is an affront to me. So highly respected; look how far he's come despite his disability. His wife is even beautiful, they say. His blue, metallic eyes fixed on me, now beyond me, show a mind steeled against me.

"You have difficulty acting spontaneously," he observed.

"Acting spontaneously? Ever try that? It's hard. I had a director once—well, more of a traffic cop, really—who preblocked all my scenes and expected a performance at first rehearsal: 'More passion, more passion,' he kept urging. You know, if you told that to your wife, you'd make her very nervous."

He rose and took a step backward, as though I'd given him a push. "Do you know how sick you are?" I had no answer. "By the way, starting tomorrow, we're locking you out of your room during the day. You're wasting too much precious time in here. And oh, yes, we'll be confiscating your pen."

"*Why?*"

"We think your writing is interfering with your therapy."

He swung around, and flipping the tail of his long, white coat, strode from the room.

The cruel acts of a kind man or retaliation for wounding his too-tender ego? I believe it the latter, but resolve not to tell him because he'll think it a persecution fantasy. It *was* a little nasty of me—spontaneous, but nasty—to compare him with that traffic cop. I wrestle again with doubts. Why am I here, if not to keep account of his barbs, to find where they are justified? Yes, this is part of the process, I decide, to show my true self for correction. I am the bitch Dr. Consultant thought me.

I cried quietly alone; it wasn't easy. I could barely squeeze out any tears at all. No sooner did they start, than I kept wishing someone would find me, and this interfered with full belief in my remorse. Miriam down the hall, a slender, auburn-haired adolescent, does something similar: she wails a wordless song to simulate her grief. She's trying to bring it up; she can't. Her vocal acrobatics annoy everyone. Someone at dinner accused her of "cultivating her madness." Oh, the martyrdom of being misjudged.

~

The next morning, as usual after our garden walk: "O.T. ladies!"

I was first in line. Almost done weaving a pair of gold, intricately patterned drapes for my future home, no sooner was I at my loom than I was told they were missing. Five months' work missing? *How*, when it's always locked up? It must have been an inside job. The occupational therapist was terribly, *terribly* sorry. I was furious enough to cry. "You're overreacting," she said.

"Is my every response inappropriate?" I burst out later to Dr. Stinta.

"I'm glad you're feeling something," he responded, "even if your feelings are unpleasant."

Throughout the rest of the day in R.T., in the garden, and on the roof, I felt a growing nervousness and hunger. A binge was on its way. By 4:30 I was ravenous; two hours till dinner! The others were setting up for bridge and Scrabble in the lounge. Locked out of my room, I sat among them. Hunger gnawed away. I roamed the corridors; the rooms were empty.

"Hi!" I exclaimed cheerfully to a tablemate. "I don't suppose you saved anything from lunch? A roll, an apple—anything?"

"Sorry."

I kept walking back and forth, peering into the empty rooms. I spied a bag of oranges on young Richard's dresser, wandered blithely in, took one, and wandered out. There he was, coming toward me! I replaced it and met him at his door.

"What are you doing in my room?" he asked.

"I'm not aware of being in your room," I replied.

"Nurse!"

"Miss Hebald, what's the meaning of this?"

"I don't know," I answered sheepishly. "Crazy people are supposed to do inappropriate things."

"Like ending up in state hospitals? Please join the others."

The following morning, with Dr. Stinta: "I'd like to request a small block of time—say two hours a day—to waste reading."

"Denied. You can't concentrate anyway."

"How do you know?" No answer. "You people behave like gods!"

"You people?"

"You heard it."

"You're lacking," he replied quietly, with a ruler.

"Because I tried to steal Richard's orange? We laughed about that later." No answer. "You know these interviews can be wearing on the patient as well as the doctor." No answer. "Yes, I prefer you when you don't speak."

"Of course. I'm criticizing you and you're not liking it."

"That's right. You make me feel there's nothing to me *but* my illness, and when I start to act accordingly, tell me I'm lacking."

"Precisely." And he left. I went into the bathroom and, with a lace from the sensible shoes Mother bought me, tried to choke myself. For this I was shipped back to Seven, where my chlorpromazine was increased to 400 milligrams a day.

Chapter Sixteen

O n Saturday morning rounds I met, as usual, with Dr. Stinta, and the chief resident, Dr. Lewis, a slight, grim-faced older man, who peered gravely at me through the windows of his glasses:

"How are you feeling?"

"Terrible," I said at last. "Please . . . let me have another doctor."

"What seems to be your difficulty with Dr. Stinta?"

"With him here?" But as usual he was staring past me. "He makes me feel terrible."

"How?" Dr. Lewis's eyes rode over me like wheels over frozen ground. *How* fell back in my mind. Chimes rang for morning activities. "You are here, Miss Hebald, not to feel better, but to get better." He rose.

"Get better, not feel better? What does that mean?" I shouted. "Christ Almighty! I've been getting double messages all my life, and you people wonder I retreat into fantasy? There's no place else to go!"

"If you don't like it at Payne Whitney, we can arrange for your transfer to another hospital. Come on, Tim."

A few minutes later, Nurse Hanni knocked at my door: "Time for the garden, Miss Hebald."

"I don't want to go."

"Fresh air! No fresh air? You have to come," she pressed quietly. I recalled the patient last week who, refusing to join the others on the roof, was strapped screaming to a chair and dragged. I followed Nurse Hanni to the elevator.

Two by two, round the garden in quiet conversation, Seven South was marching. I circled the walk alone behind the inseparable delinquents. "Pretty, isn't it?" said one, pointing to a neatly clipped flower bed. "*Aw*fully nice," said the other. They were noticing nature for their social skills on a morning in early November. I felt chilled. A young swallow skipped from the limb of a tree and flew over the high wall beyond. And I heard my misery in the crying of the wind.

At lunch Nurse Hanni surprised me with the news that I'd been scheduled for a staff interview the following Monday. "Don't be nervous," she warned.

"What about?"

~

"Come in, please, Miss Hebald," urged Dr. Eggertson, ushering me before a seated assembly of some twenty-five interns. I recognized Bernice's resident, stout, gentle Dr. Steinhardt, in the back row; and beside him, a recent addition to the staff, a boyish, pink-cheeked doctor whose slight sneer of complacency I'd first noted in his sympathetic glances at us along the corridors, a sympathy tinged somehow with superiority—of the well for the sick.

"I suppose you're all wondering why I've gathered you together here today," I began quietly.

No one laughed. I shifted my weight.

"Have a chair," said Dr. Eggertson, finally shoving one over.

"Thank you." And I sat down.

"Miss Hebald, will you begin by telling us exactly why you think you're here—at Payne Whitney."

"I *am* here."

A slight bow: "I see;—and why were you sent here?"

"I have a tendency to kill myself," I muttered quietly.

"Can you elaborate on that?" asked a slender young intern, pencil poised high.

"Hold it, Stingle!" intercepted Eggertson sharply. Then to me, "Do you feel yourself making progress in conquering this 'tendency'?"

"I made some intellectual progress right after my last attempt," I replied wearily. "Or I hope I did."

"Do you feel yourself progressing toward any other goal—general or particular?" he went on coolly.

"Which?"

"Whichever."

"Frankly, no. I'm afraid I don't have the social ambitions you all assume. And being forced to relate the way we are . . ." I crossed my legs and leaned back. "Well, I just can't seem to rise [I really meant lower myself] to it. Not that I don't like the people," I hastened to add. "In fact, I might go to them more easily if I weren't . . . watched."

"You relate to no one?" someone called out.

"What floor are you on?" from someone else.

Eggertson's hand shot up. "Hold it! *Please!*" Back to me: "What have you learned here?"

"I've learned that we're all human."

"Didn't you know that before?"

"Only intellectually."

"And now? That is, what altered your intellectual assumption into . . . sheer conviction?"

I leaned forward: "It was you fellas. You drummed it into me."

Did a shadow of a smile cross his lips, or did I only imagine it?

"How would you describe your relationship with Dr. Stinta?" he pressed on. "Do you find it problematic?" He cocked his head. "More problematic perhaps than therapeutic?" Now, with a jowly,

189

manufactured charm: "Or basically perhaps, more thera-peu—?"

"Sorry, I don't know where your 'basically' begins or ends."

"How do you *feel* in your relationship with Dr. Stinta?"

"I feel that he's persecuting me," I answered simply.

"And why?" Two pencils started scratching.

"I don't know, doctor. Perhaps you'd better ask him."

"I'm asking you."

"I find him cruel. I feel he's beating me—beating me with words."

"Beating you with words," echoed Eggertson thoughtfully. There was a pause. "With what words do you feel yourself being beaten?" he persisted.

"What words?"

"Yes."

And suddenly I couldn't remember. I couldn't remember! Barbara's threat from my childhood: "And if you tell about this, I'll kill you" echoed in my mind. But then, nothing.

"Yes, Miss Hebald?"

"I'm sorry?"

"What *words?*"

What stopped me up was the knowledge, certain as the memory fled, that Dr. Stinta had suffered wounds too grievous to heal and with that I identified too well. And at the expense of my sanity, that *he* had taught me to distrust, I crept quietly back into the closet. His "beatings" became my paranoia.

"Miss Hebald seems to be preoccupied again," observed Dr. Eggertson. And with that, the examination ended.

A little while later, Bernice came into our room in tears. Proust in hand, I pretended not to notice. She looked straight at me. Didn't I see her? "Carol?"

"What?" I snarled in my sister's harshest voice. She turned away. I walked out hating her, hating her for crying because I couldn't. No more tender feelings inside me. They're there, but I can't reach them—can't reach in or out. I'm guilty for cutting her. I want to tell her I'm sorry.

The interview went badly; I knew it. Couldn't I have conceded that the clinic was probably keeping me alive, that in pushing me to relate, Dr. Stinta had probably meant well? Yesterday Flossy was skipped down to Five because *she* knows how to behave. Her manner all but says it: a good patient is gracious and grateful for every professional offering, no matter its merits. If she doesn't understand her doctor's judgments, she must thank him nonetheless for making them. When he tries her with verbal stickpins in order to provoke her rage, she must know he doesn't want it; that's why he drives it inside, with pricks, prods, and pills, where in time it will go automatically.

Under the heap of past suffering we are building a pile for the future. That's why we keep returning. And why Lucia, down on Six, let out on pass last weekend, took her life. And my God! I just realized now that I never tried to take mine before I began therapy. But then, moving along the spotless green carpet, I don't know why I'm so perfectly filled with hate for Dr. Eggertson and all his cohorts. For I do not admit exceptions among them.

"Good morning!" called Dr. Peterson, approaching me in his slow, rigid, mechanical walk.

"Good morning," I answered and kept moving.

"Please!" someone cried from her bedroom. "Have some respect for me as a person as well as a mental patient! I studied psychology, too."

"You're acting up again," reminded her doctor sharply.

It was not that I resolved to act appropriately but, little by little, was broken into it. I had no pressing desire to leave; this misery was comfortable. I still enjoyed taking medications, even from Dr. Stinta.

~

Last night Iris was permitted to sleep in her regular bed. She spoke neither to Bernice nor to me. She looked pale and frightened. At three this morning, she began shouting. Two aides rushed in; she dodged them and ran out. When they caught her, they put her in restraints and took her away again.

All day she's been on my mind: the who and the what and the why of that lovely, whey-faced child. Those huge, starved eyes. I feel pity for her, true pity, from which all contempt is absent. But I keep it to myself.

"No roof for us this afternoon," sighed Nurse O'Brien at lunch today. "It's pouring out."

"Oh, I'm so sorry," I lied sincerely. "I was looking forward to going," and received her first warm smile.

"The whole goddamned world is raving about my book, but my doctor complains it's too depressing," lamented Arthur.

"You can't win 'em all, Arthur," I said pleasantly.

"Oh, don't you think so, Carol? You want to fight?"

"Sure, I want to fight."

"Then stand up and put up your fists."

I stood up and put up my fists. "Now what am I supposed to do?"

"Punch me." He gulped down his string bean.

"I can't."

"Why not?"

"I'm not mad at you."

"Nurse, she's crazy," he hollered.

"Arthur, why are you so mean?"

"How old are you, Miss Hebald?" asked Nurse Hanni, setting down our dessert tray.

"Gee, I'm not sure, Nurse, but I can tell you where to look it up."

Her testy glance lingered a moment. Am I feeling better or just faking it? But that I have the energy to fake it must mean I'm on my way.

"Golf on the green?" asked Arthur, after silvercheck.

"Golf on the green?" I echoed.

"On the green carpet," he explained. "The aides are setting up down the hall with balls and broomsticks."

Only a few more such friendly encounters under the watchful eye of the staff, and I was transferred back to Six, along with Phipsy, Stephanie, and Mrs. Fine.

Iris was shipped to a state hospital. She was making too much of a fuss.

~

"He *couldn't* be twenty-five," exclaimed Phipsy the next night at nourishment.

"He *is!*" insisted Martha. "He's a genius."

"She should know," said Mrs. Fine, munching a graham cracker.

Martha was a brilliant student who'd still be in class if this *thing* hadn't overtaken her. "Did you see him today?" she asked Stephanie.

"Uh-huh."

"How long did he keep you?"

"Thirty-four minutes—exactly. You?"

"Thirty-two—exactly."

"Who are you talking about?" I asked finally.

"The new resident, Dr. Traynor."

"The blonde with the pink cheeks?"

"Yes," answered Mrs. Fine, sipping her tea. "Ooooh, he's so adorable I could just pinch him."

"He cares," said Martha.

"He really cares," echoed Stephanie.

"He can be very loving," repeated Martha quietly.

The clinic ambled through its days, sweeping us off to activities, as mood and weather dictated. Flossy had been dismissed, and Arthur skipped down to Five. I'd long since stopped talking to Dr. Stinta. Mother, back from a cruise with Charles, told the clinic she'd run out of funds. And I became a free patient. Soon after, I received news that I'd been reassigned to the new resident.

On an early Monday morning in January, he knocked on my half-opened door.

"Come in!" I glanced up from my notebook.

He was so young! A sweet whisper of down shaded his upper lip. He wore his stiff white hospital coat a little awkwardly for a genius. I was grateful.

"Miss Hebald? I'm Dr. Traynor." And pulling over a chair, "What are you writing?" he asked.

"Nothing much. 'Fresh hot tea in a clean white cup.' I'm waiting for the second line."

"Have you written stuff before?"

"A little."

∾

Always I looked forward to my meetings with Dr. Traynor and would share my poems with him. In time he let me go out alone for neighborhood walks. One day, strolling along the nearby East River, I found my second line—a lifeline is what it felt like. The next time I brought pad and pencil. At night, when Dr. Traynor was on call, I'd wait anxiously for him in my room. It bothered me that he spent so much time with other patients. The evening I found courage to admit it:

"If you were happier, people would like you better," he ventured.

"That doesn't mean much to me."

"It means more than you think."

Each time I saw him I felt on a slightly higher rung of hell than the day before. I began weaving him a tie in O.T., and shed the weight I'd gained; it was so easy! And I became a little friendlier with the others. Martha kept asking if I'd fallen in love yet, and seeing the yes in my smile, told Stephanie, who was perfectly furious. *She* was Traynor's most interesting; *she* wasn't sick: she'd downed a heavy underdose of Seconal and came here, she claimed, just from "intellectual curiosity."

"Why are you always so quiet?" asked Dr. Traynor.

"If I admit it, you'll be embarrassed."

"Admit it, let me be embarrassed."

"I feel tongued-tied because . . . I like you."

He smiled. "I like you, too."

In O. T. I was blinded by the rhythm of the spinning wheel. The threads of his tie got tangled. I stopped to straighten them out. I had a friend. The blue-green threads were dancing. My mind was dancing. The nurse was watching; I hid my face. She wrote something down in her pad. Who cared? I'd learn everything now in an instant, get well for him, only for him. He loves me—how can he help himself? I laughed out loud. Shhhh, I told myself. Spin, spin, spin. I was happy for the first time in years—happy, awkwardly happy—like a chick just out of the egg.

One day, finding me as usual following the words in Proust, he asked, "Ever read mysteries, just for fun?"

"Sure."

"Which ones?"

Quick! Think of a title. He's trying to get me to enjoy myself, to remind me as he will until the day I leave, that Nobody Loves a Sad Sack.

"I don't remember any mystery titles," I admitted finally. Then, "Why is it wrong to improve my mind?"

"I didn't say it was wrong." He crossed his legs. "I just don't see why you do all that heavy reading when there's no one here to discuss it with."

"I don't read Proust for my social skills," I announced proudly. "And I wouldn't discuss him, even if there were a Proust scholar among us." At which he raised an eyebrow. "I'm not ready! I've never read him before."

And because Dr. Traynor hadn't either, I told him that reading Proust is like listening to great music. In a Bach fugue for example, I'm crossing fields of thought I have no desire to share with any third party because I'm in an intimate relationship with the composer. "Listening, really listening, is like working the soil with him. Images and phrases come to me from that."

Dr. Traynor "appreciated" my feelings, then suggested reasonably that I didn't know what sharing was, and wouldn't until I tried it. He wasn't well versed in art, but what about munching roasted chestnuts with a loved one on a winter night, spending all day Sunday in bed? Yes, yes, yes, I cried inwardly. Well, the opportunity to share was sitting right before me. "Why don't you tell me your fantasies about me?"

"Well," I began. "I pretend that after I'm out, we . . . we become friends. That's all."

"That's all?" He smiled.

"Well no. What happens is . . . we meet on a crowded bus.

We're standing side by side, hanging onto the straps; the bus lurches. I land on your feet, and we start fighting."

He laughed gaily. "You feel like fighting now?"

"Yes."

"Why?"

"Because I hate you."

He laughed again. "Go on. What happens then?"

"We recognize each other from here."

"And? Do we go to bed?"

"I don't know. If we get to know each other and want to, I guess so. I mean I hope so. Why?"

He jotted something down and rose quickly. "You're doing much better," he said. "You're beginning to relate."

"Wait! I want to give you something. I found it in the library. It's short—could you read it? It's very beautiful."

I handed him Herman Melville's story "Bartleby the Scrivener."*

~

"He's obviously schizophrenic," said Dr. Traynor at the beginning of our next interview.

"Who's schizophrenic?"

"Bartleby," he replied, handing me the book.

"Doctor, you're not doing it right," I said.

"Doing what?" he asked, a little puzzled.

"Relating."

Why? Because "Bartleby" is literature, not case history, and in saying so, I anticipate a little because I didn't know then how

---

*This nineteenth-century story concerns a copyist who takes refuge from the hostile world of Wall Street behind the walled-in windows of an office in which he lives but refuses to work.

strongly I felt this, only that Dr. Traynor's comment had offended me, and I him.

The next morning in O.T., determined to finish his tie, I wove furiously against the clock. Did I honestly feel, or think I ought to feel, ashamed of myself? I bit off a hanging thread and laughed at the stupidity of oughting myself to feel anything except that I loved him and was very sorry I'd hurt him. At chimes, I breathed a sigh of relief. I had just finished.

I took the tie downstairs, along with several other projects I'd been urged to take with me, as I was hogging too much storage space. I laid my projects neatly on the bed and waited for Dr. Traynor.

He arrived ten minutes late, and glancing impatiently at my bed, asked, "What's all this?"

"My O.T. projects."

He saw three evening purses; one of crewel embroidery, two of the same golden weave as my stolen drapes, three angora winter scarves, a trivet, an ashtray, two sculptures, and his tie.

"Very nice," he said.

"Thank you. Here, this is for you." I handed him his tie. He fingered its rough weave in silence. I was about to suggest he try it on at my washstand mirror. "I'm sorry, I can't accept this," he said.

I took it back and, head averted, replaced it on the bed. He peered around at me and caught my eye. "You look like you've just been slapped in the face," he observed, and waited for a response. I gathered together my projects.

"You work like a fiend upstairs, don't you?"

"I enjoy it."

"How would you feel about finding a real job?"

"Am I being dismissed?" I asked quickly.

"Not yet. But we can't keep you here forever, you know."

"What kind of job?"

"Clerical? Secretarial?"

"I can't type."

"We have a practice machine upstairs in O.T."

I'd still use the hospital for meals, board, and therapy, but I'd be expected to job hunt in the morning and practice typing in the afternoons. In addition, I'd be let out for a few hours on weekends for planned social activities.

Rising to leave, he added, "You'll be expected to return right afterward. We don't want you wandering the streets just to wait out your pass time."

Chapter Seventeen

*M*y mood dropped sharply. I had never before liked a young man, and here was one who awakened my longing, only to warn it away. Resolved not to outstay my welcome, I continued to practice on the typewriter and soon landed a part-time secretarial spot at *This Week* Magazine. When Mother called Dr. Traynor to say how absolutely delighted she was that I'd finally "gone into business in a high-class office," I thanked him for relaying the message.

"You seem to be having trouble adjusting to your role as secretary," he remarked. The subtext was clear: who did I think I was?

On weekends, I'd cut short my visits to Mother and Charles in Jersey City and ride the New York subways or walk the streets. One rainy Saturday I stood for a long time watching the tiny, crested waves on the East River, when the image sailed into my mind: "Many-nippled river of the night." The line insisted itself into a poem, the first among many to come.

In March I joined Stephanie and Martha down on Five, and my release date was set for April 1.

One Monday morning at work, I read in the paper that the producer Herman Shumlin was casting extras for a Broadway show. I ran over to the theater at lunchtime and found Mr. Shumlin just leaving:

"Sorry, Miss Hebald," he said, hurriedly glancing past me. "You're too late."

My decision to give up acting, a heart change as sudden as it was irrevocable, followed on the heels of this incident. How, at thirty, I could forfeit in an instant what had been the object and reward of my existence for two decades I don't know. The straw that broke my back was needle sharp: a producer who'd remembered me from better days now thought nothing of rejecting me as an extra. Dr. Traynor was stunned at my news. "I've had enough! Enough humiliation," was all I told him. There had to be something else. My practice hours at the typewriter would not be wasted. The next morning I wrote to cousin Milton in Rome, asking if he knew of a writing teacher I might try with samples of my work.

"How do you feel about leaving?" asked Dr. Traynor at our last in-hospital interview.

"Frightened, not ready. I want to go, and I don't."

"I'll still be your doctor," he reassured. "But you'll have to pay my outpatient fee—fifty cents a session."

I smiled. "Why do *you* think I'm ready?"

"Frankly? You're difficult to diagnose. I'm baffled," he said finally. "I wouldn't know how to categorize you!"

Baffled, was he? Because I didn't fit a certain set of predetermined symptoms? His discharge diagnosis classified them predictably enough as "schizophrenic—chronic undifferentiated type," a mixed form of the disease (prognosis guarded). In which case, went my thoughts, I'd confound him further by thriving. But whether I'd succeed remained to be seen.

The night before I left, the main entrée for dinner was roast chicken. I ate five quarters, six well-buttered baked potatoes, all the extra peas in the pot, three tall, friendly glasses of milk, and a large hunk of chocolate cake topped with vanilla ice cream. "I'm still hungry," I announced, laying down my fork. "I want more cake."

"It's made with Ajax," said Martha.

"I still want it."

"Well, they won't give it to you. Rules, remember? One dessert."

"Why?"

"They want you to understand that in life on the outside, you won't get too much of a sweet thing."

"She gathered that," commented Stephanie.

On April 1, 1964, I was dismissed to a halfway house.

I'll skim over the next year and a half, a hell redeemed only by my efforts to define on the page, no matter how badly, the images in my mind. I never wrote of the realities around me or thought since of my months in that converted brownstone on a lovely, tree-lined street in Chelsea, where house therapist Libby saw to it that we job hunted or worked during the day. Drug addicts, ex-convicts, convalescing mental patients, we'd join her in the common room after dinner to share problems. Each time she caught me sneaking off to read, she'd protest, "There you go withdrawing again."

The night one of the ex-convicts put a cat in the oven, I left without notice. Dialing Payne Whitney from the corner booth before Libby had a chance to report me, I phoned back an hour later to say I'd taken a room with a hot plate at an Upper West Side hotel. There, weeks later, Milton's reply to my letter reached me with the advice that I send my poems to Professor Alfred Grunwald at CCNY (the City College of New York). At summer's end Professor Grunwald and I spoke at my hotel.

Of upright, portentous posture, with opaque hazel eyes and a ski-slope nose, Alfred at forty-six had the bearing of a distinguished man of letters. He judged my work full of feeling; I'd evidently been "hurt in the right places," but had absolutely no conception of craft. Had I ever considered going to college? No, but

I would now. Could he in the meantime please give me a list of books to read?

I was working as a full-time secretary and had moved to a studio apartment when Alfred invited me to audit his evening graduate course in American literature. I watched intently his stance at the blackboard, cigarette poised gracefully in hand, as he pounced on student theses: "Where do you find that in the text?" he grilled. This might have been the feel-creative sixties, but no student of his would read between the lines without considering the words themselves. How otherwise find the spaces between them? "That's why an A from Grunwald means something," he'd boast modestly to me afterward.

I had missed one class when his prompt note of concern followed. Alfred had fallen in love, and assuming I felt the same, warned me that he wouldn't leave his wife and children. I didn't want him to! He was my friend. For this alone I was grateful.

In the summer of '65, I enrolled as a special student in CCNY's evening session, where for freshman English and music I received A's. Alfred urged me to matriculate. As my C average in high school disqualified me from the more rigorous day session, I'd have to work my way in. I began as a full-time evening student that fall, when Alfred went off to England on a Fulbright.

Curiosity became the appetite of my intellect, and learning my bread of life. Did I know how lucky I was to be able to study round the clock? Mother paid my rent: it was cheap; I lived cheaply. One of the ways I managed my close-to-straight-A average was to lighten my fall and spring semester loads by taking six summer school credits each year. I read everything, assigned and unassigned. Finding Spenser's *The Faerie Queene* omitted from our Fall English Survey syllabus, I spent the end of that first summer reading it on my own. "Can't you read for fun?" persisted Dr. Traynor. It was such torturous fun, I wouldn't even go for walks. "You have to walk," he said.

Instead, I stayed home like a child disgraced, and for spite made use of my time. I had left the theater determined to make it somewhere. On this nothing, no one would intrude. But forbidding myself distractions yet again would mark me the fool. Though I'd been exempted from English 2, the B-minus I received for my first in-class sophomore English essay plunged me into such despair, I downed a bottle of sleeping pills. How I got to St. Vincent's hospital to have my stomach pumped I don't know, but I do remember Dr. Traynor's righteous fury when he visited. "Thanks," he said bitterly, "for trying it on *my* prescription."

Not long after he went into private practice, and I was reassigned, still a free patient, to Payne Whitney's Dr. Leon Klewes.

⁓

Short, erect, with a long upper lip and a well-hung, bullish jaw, Dr. Klewes spoke at first almost exclusively about himself. I guessed it was his way of warming up. He was married with a newborn baby, whose screams he couldn't endure. "Babies are so incredibly self-centered," he complained. Frankly, he preferred his dog. "Dogs are so uncomplicated!" But he had a problem: his was vicious. It bit all his friends, and he didn't know what to do. Did I have a dog? Why didn't I get one? I bought a little dachshund at Gimbel's, and named him Tibi. Why didn't I bring Tibi to our talks? It was still warm; we could sit outside on the grounds. No, I came straight from school. It would be awkward.

"Are you managing to attend your classes?" he asked one day.

"I'm a dedicated student. I don't skip classes," I replied more sharply than I meant.

A brief pause. "You don't like me much, do you?"

"I'm sorry. I was close to Dr. Traynor. It's hard to make the change."

That fall, Alfred returned from England and we made love for the first time. Tossing the blankets from my body, "Such loveliness!" he exclaimed. "Where do I come off?" The Bronx accent I'd once found charming began suddenly to grate on my nerves. I balked at his frequent phone calls. It bothered me that he loved me; what did he love me for? I had made no secret of my history, trusting him to keep it to himself. But when, despite my objections, he persisted in discussing me with his best friend and colleague, Michael, whose responses he relayed back to me ("Aw, come on, we tell each other everything"), I protested to Dr. Klewes.

"But I thought you liked being the center of attention!" responded Klewes.

"Why, because I was an actress? Look, I'm grateful for Alfred's interest in my poems." Then I admitted the truth. I more-than-liked Michael, whose warm greetings on campus I'd replay each night in my mind. A divorced man—bald, chubby—he limped ever so slightly on an elevated heel. His shyness moved me, his kind face resembled my father's. Alfred knew my feelings

"You're a lousy mistress, you know that?" interrupted Klewes.

"What?"

"You're not living up to your responsibilities."

"I don't understand."

"You need every friend you can get."

"I've heard *that* before," I conceded. "In fact, I might have more in common with you in this area than with Dr. Traynor."

"How so?" his ears perked up.

"Well, the child in you often comes through to me. So much so that I've had fantasies about you as a little boy being abused, just as I was, by your playmates."

205

I said it because he offended me, but I hadn't *felt* it maliciously; it was just something I sensed we shared. But I'd said more than I should. He was never the same with me after. The following week, having come to him straight from school, I was told he had an inpatient emergency and would be with me soon. I waited an hour and a half, left him a note, and went home.

Next time: "What you did was incredibly self-centered."

"I was hungry!"

A just-perceptible pause. "You're entirely predictable," he declared. I shrugged in response. "You have absolutely no respect for anything I say!"

Because I didn't know what to do with a perception like that! Predictable because I got hungry at meal times? I had work to do, too. Did I imagine mine as important as his? You bet. Then why didn't I say so? Couldn't I phrase the thought? Why always did I consent to be brought to trial on charges I didn't understand? I was thought to *know* nothing, to *be* nothing; retarded in the ways of the world, a pawn of circumstance left back by time. Dr. Stinta had judged me "lacking"; Klewes, "incredibly self-centered." My former therapists had all agreed. So anxious to find what was wrong with me, they couldn't see anything right. But much was right, and I knew it. Slowly, oh so slowly, I was beginning to gather strength, and simply didn't realize that my want of respect for their thinking was too absolute to hide. I never mastered respect as a social skill, that is, the pretense of respect as a means of evading control.

The day I admitted my adoration for Michael—I could think now of no one else—Dr. Klewes snickered in my face. "What's funny?" I asked. "The intensity," he replied. Didn't I understand that it all came down to the loss of my father at an age when all little girls worship their fathers? Omitting my experience of incest—and why now did he choose to omit it?—was there no more to it than that? No more to a feeling that could strike and drive me forth from despair to life? No more *because* it was mere feeling? Or because it left him out?

When I repeated to Alfred Klewes's complaint, "Why can't you be as creative in therapy as you seem to be in your poetry?" Alfred exclaimed, "Exactly!"

Auditing his English class one evening, I heard him censure an immoral fictional character as an adulterer. Noting his hypocrisy, I never suspected how harshly I censured myself for a pleasure I could have done without. That I paid penance in despair was still inconceivable to me; I didn't know its cause. To Dr. Klewes it was symptomatic of my illness.

"Your thinking is psychotic," he remarked. I was prompted to ask my diagnosis. "Paranoid schizophrenic," he told me openly (no other doctor had). He gave me his home phone number. "Use it when you need it." This I thought most generous, until I needed it too much.

A few weeks later: "You've called me three times this month on a Sunday," he snarled. "You're abusing the privilege of calling me at home." I was devastated. The fault was mine entirely. I wouldn't bother him again.

After all my years in therapy, I knew enough to expect the usual quizzes on what happened between my father and me the year before he died. But what intrigued Dr. Klewes were the feelings these memories evoked.

"You recall no fear? No dread?"

"Pleasure only," I said wearily. "I told you that."

"How do you feel about your body?" he asked.

"Fine—when I'm thin. Why?"

"But most women hate their bodies!"

"But? I'm not most women, I'm me."

"And most women don't have bodies like yours," he added.

The following week he had some extra time on his hands: was I free? Yes. He began by asking whether I'd ever had sexual fantasies about him. It was a usual question, most doctors asked it. I hemmed and hawed. "They're not only about you," I said. "My early memories are still with me: in the movies, alleyways, under the boardwalk. Usually I pretend I'm with strangers. I still have to separate sex from love."

"I know, I know. What fantasies?" He uncapped his pen.

I began to relay them. "Wow!" he exclaimed, jotting them down. I went on. "Wow!" again. He continued to write. Would we be done soon? Not yet. I hardly recall what I said. Three hours is rather a long time to keep anyone entertained, but then imagination is my strong point. Finally, he recapped his pen and rose.

"I don't want to go to bed with you after all," he concluded. "You're too sick for me."

"I didn't realize I was *for* you at all."

"But you were for Dr. Traynor, weren't you?"

"What are you talking about?"

"You offered yourself to him, didn't you?"

"What? My God! Did he tell you that? I loved him. He asked for my fantasies like you did." I stopped. The fantasy I'd shared with Traynor was of our accidental meeting on a bus. And when I admitted wanting to sleep with him, he told me I was doing much better. He knew I'd been promiscuous. But how he could rub my nose in my past—a past I'd stumbled into from sheer need . . . Did these bastards know the meaning of need? No, no they were different. Traynor couldn't have told such a lie. But Klewes could. To him I was guilty of my appetite.

But my promiscuity had ended long ago. What was happening? Who was I to Klewes? Some brutal woman in his past who had hurt him? Or had I myself piqued his vanity so often he couldn't help biting back? The man was ill; I should report him—to whom? Given my diagnosis, who'd believe me? He left me no cheek to turn, no face to save. I sat upright, still, every movement a source of pain, even altering my gaze.

"You're posturing," he said finally.

"What?"

"Your limbs are beginning to lock. Just a minute."

He left briefly and returned with some fat pill. "Can you swallow it without water?" There was a fountain outside, but he seemed to enjoy watching me struggle to swallow. When I had: "It'll give relief in a while. Here," he offered, "take the whole packet."

"What's happening?" I asked.

"You're on a masochistic binge."

That I didn't know he was feeding it. That I didn't know!

Next day was Thursday. I ran into Alfred on campus. Remarking on my pallor, he asked what was wrong.

"Nothing. I'm on some new pill."

"See you later? Where are you going?"

"Across the street to Psychological Counseling."

"You're not going to tell them about us, are you?"

I didn't know what I'd say. There was a wait to see the doctor. I stayed ten minutes and left.

"What happened there?" asked Alfred, as soon as he entered my door.

"Nothing. I just rested."

"What'sa matter, babe?"

He sat beside me on the couch, expounding on the pitfalls of despair. On and on he droned. I wanted him to go home; I couldn't say it. Finally he was done. "No tea for us today?" he asked. I got up to make it. "That schizophrenic walk," he exclaimed softly.

"Did you have to say that to me?"

"Yes! More . . . let me know more how you feel!" Silence. He drank his tea. "You'd rather have Michael here, wouldn't you?"

"I suppose he knows it, too."

"Of course."

"I don't understand it," I admitted. "I hardly know him."

"*I* understand it. He's single; I'm not."

"And?"

"He doesn't want anyone that sick." The tears came—I couldn't stop them. "Oh, my poor girl." He put his arm around me and waited. "Not done yet? Oh, child!" He drew me closer. My misery seemed always to excite him. His breathing grew heavy. "I have to take you now," he said.

At my door: "Remember all those A's."

I walked Tibi to the kennel. With me was a prepaid check for his boarding and a full bottle of sleeping pills. After depositing him, I downed the pills in the kennel bathroom. A spring rain was falling. One last walk? No, there might not be time. I hailed a cab, but traffic was slow. Next morning I awoke in Bellevue and thought I was in hell.

~

No doors in the stalls of the ladies' room. A woman sits on the toilet. Another passes by.

"Jackass!" she mutters.

"Who you callin' jackass, Jackass?"

"You the jackass settin' there scratchin' yo' black pussy."

"Watch it! Here come whitie! Asked me this mornin' 'Where

am I?' 'Lady,' I says, 'you is on the Suicide Unit of our free city hospital.'"

The climate of oblivion is mildewed. Mice flit about like confused functionaries under the cots that line the corridor walls. Above mine is a captioned poster of a black woman weeping in agony: "Tell me *how!*" Last night, when I got up for a drink of water, "Where d' ya think you're goin'?" screamed a cleaning lady with a broom.

"Don't yell at me," I sobbed like a two-year-old.

This morning on our breakfast queue, fat Leda sat on her Hershey bar and cried. At the front was a huge pot of yellowing hard-boiled eggs. "One each, ladies!" someone shouted like a circus barker. A young woman behind me, too weak to stand on her feet, sank to the floor. "Yolanda, get up," someone ordered. "All I want is a cup o' coffee," she whined. I offered to bring it to her. "No, they only let you take one."

"One egg, ladies!"

After breakfast our entire ward is herded into a dayroom twice the size of Gracie Square's. Light is admitted by windows with massive iron bars. The nailed-down benches are all taken. A buzzing florescent light glares. All morning I sit against the wall with Yolanda's head in my lap. "My huzbin' was driving up near the Hun'-Eighty-first Street bridge. I asked him to stop. 'Cause I hadda buy stockin's, I told him. Then I made a run for it. But he caught me. Wouldn' lemme go—wouldn' lemme."

"You going to do it when you leave?" I ask.

"*If.*"

"What about your children?"

"My children will be all right."

Saturday morning. Fat Leda eats her Hershey bar for breakfast. Dr. Rosenberg passes jauntily through: "Hey, Rosenberg," she hollers.

"Yeah?"

"*Gut Yuntif** and go fuck yourself."

He laughs, she laughs—we all laugh.

At Saturday afternoon showers, no towels. "Dry yourselves with your dresses, ladies. You catch a cold, we fix it."

That night, we attend a dance with the criminally insane upstairs. They wear robes; we, our loose, damp hospital dresses. The music is blaring. I'm sitting against the wall, when a six-foot hulk sidles over: "Come on." I don't dare refuse.

"You can't dance!" he hollers.

"Neither can you!"

He laughs, I laugh—we all laugh.

Sunday, I'm sobbing on the phone to Dr. Klewes, "Please visit me."

"I don't know whether I will or not."

~

That night Leda and I lay awake. "You have a cigarette?" I asked. "I ran out."

"It's after smoking hours. Oh, here." She gave me one. "Wait." She reached into her pillow for matches.

"Thank you! Where the hell did you get . . . ?"

"Shhhhh! Light it on the toilet seat. If a nurse comes, douse it and take a Sen-Sen. Got one? Here. Come back after!"

We talked all night. She's a student, too—fat, pockmarked, funny. In the morning, she'd be dragged screaming again to the state hospital: Rosenberg's orders.

After she left, I called Alfred at home: we can't make long-

---

*Yiddish for "Good Sabbath."

distance calls. Would he please phone my mother in Jersey City and ask her to sign me out?

Doing so against medical advice, she told Dr. Rosenberg at the door, "Carol'll be a good girl now, and you be a good boy."

Outside I thanked her and kissed her cheek. Mother manages everything.

~

"There's no doubt in my mind you'll take your own life," said Dr. Klewes at our next interview. "It's only a question of time."

He was writing me a new prescription, which he neglected to sign. I left several messages for him at the clinic that day and the next. He never returned my calls. Finally reaching him at home, I was furious enough to cross swords:

"Why didn't you call me back? You get a signed prescription to me immediately or—"

"If you need medication right away, you go to the emergency room," he roared back.

"Why didn't your secretary tell me that? Why do you make me chase after you for your mistake? Would you treat a private patient like this?"

The following week: "How dare you beat up on me like a member of your family?"

"A member of my family? If you can't stand a little justified rage, doctor, I suggest you get some help yourself. What the hell is this process for?"

"You'll never know," he said. "You're hopeless."

"Because you can't help me?"

"Your life is frightening."

"What a babyboo!"

That week, as if by magic, the good news tumbled in: I'd been placed on the Dean's List, invited into the day session, and encouraged to apply to the English honors program. Though I had in the meantime contacted another therapist, I kept my final appointment with Dr. Klewes, who skulked in an hour late. I knocked on his door.

"Did you forget?" I asked.

"I didn't think you'd return after last time," he muttered.

"Not return without calling? I've come to say good-bye. I'll be seeing another doctor now."

"Very responsible of you to tell me."

"I'm a very responsible person."

I relayed my news; it *was,* after all, why I'd come.

"You'll do well for a while," he conceded grudgingly. "You're talented, attractive—not unpleasantly Jewish."

"Well, aren't you sweet?" I murmured. "As for you, I think you have a great deal of work to do before you can hope to treat any-one."

"You're incredible," he said.

"You think so? Not very happy are you? I never met a happy sadist; you're no exception to that. Entirely predictable, in fact. Get off on three hours of sex fantasies, then present me with a malicious lie? How *could* you use my past against me—a past *you* should have helped me to shed?"

"Lower your voice!"

"Why? Scared someone'll hear? You pathetic son of a bitch, you're as vicious and cowardly as your dog."

"Absolutely incredible!"

"Thank you."

I rose, smiled graciously, and for an instant saw him turning on the spit.

Chapter Eighteen

*T*here was no doubt in Dr. Klewes's mind that I'd take my own life, so for spite I decided to save it. Do I owe it to him, then? If so, my worst enemy is my friend because he spurred me on to fight. I was aware, as never before, of the spiteful streak in my nature. But to make of this sorry characteristic a happy fault, to spite *for good cause,* as I'd first done inadvertently in high school when, in response to Mother's indifference to my grades ("All you want is to pass"), I resolved secretly to do better: this was my object now.

I'll pass quickly over the years between my graduation from City College and my first full-time teaching job, lonely, happy years filled with the rewards and pleasures of hard work. The doctors who maintained me were proud of my accomplishments. None would shame me with impunity again.

At City College I had won, along with academic honors, both the poetry and fiction awards, and was granted a Teaching and Writing Fellowship in Fiction Writing at the University of Iowa's Writers' Workshop. While I was there, Loree Rackstraw, the editor of *North American Review* (NAR), accepted an excerpt from my novella *Asylum.* The afternoon she drove in from Cedar Falls to Iowa City to meet me, I knew I'd found a friend. My novella *Clara Kleinschmidt* was under way when I was offered an English instructorship at the University of Northern Iowa, where Loree taught. She found me an apartment right around the corner from her house. We'd be neighbors—Loree, her husband, the poet and professor Dick Rackstraw, and their five children from former marriages. So in 1971 I took my MFA degree, moved to Cedar Falls, and prepared my classes.

I taught the short story that year, not very well I'm afraid. Still on heavy medication, I couldn't think on my feet. Nor could I trust myself to lecture from note cards; my mind was too apt to wander or, worse, stop in its tracks. So I wrote out my lectures and read them as spontaneously as I could.

In addition, I was assigned a course in argument—a windfall because I had to read the daily paper, from which students chose such topics as, for example, "Capital punishment is no deterrent to crime: yes or no? Why?" I suggested they consider their confusions. Those who admitted none I urged to consider mine. Heated discussions followed. It was my most exciting class. I continued to write; my poems were coming out in first-rate literary journals. And Loree had accepted *Clara Kleinschmidt* for *NAR*.

All this while I was seeing a therapist she had recommended, the psychologist Melville Finkelstein in nearby Waterloo.

As I meet him from the distance of memory—his great mop of curly red hair mingled with threads of gray, his calm, penetrating gaze, his abiding warmth and gravity—I realize I loved him from the start. And because he was the first doctor in or out of hospital to help me, I want to remember my time with him in some detail.

After hearing about my therapeutic experiences, he conceded, "I can understand why you went to so many doctors, but when you saw yourself standing still, *why did you stay?*"

"I didn't know I was standing still; they told me progress is as hard for the doctor to chart as it is for the patient to feel."

"But when you began slipping backward?"

"They said regression is part of the process. They forbade me to read in the area, you know. I never went beyond Psych One in college."

"Obedient little girl. Didn't you ask them why?"

Again, why did I submit to their savagery?

"I couldn't trust my instincts, even in the face of knowing better, that I was being punished. That I was more than the sum of my maladies, I knew. But I was afraid to leave, afraid I'd fall apart alone. They made me feel so sick, I thought treatment was all of human intercourse I could have." I was silent a moment. Then, "One thing I know: being forced into a closet is nothing to the psychic labor pains of being forced out."

"Because you don't remember it? Why were you forced in?"

I had indeed forgotten.

Dr. Finkelstein never asked for my feelings, but let them come at their will. When finally I told him I loved him, he said he knew, but it was nothing to feel anxious about. Of course, I jumped instantly to the importance of my work.

"Look, you're a person first," he began.

"No!" I cried in protest.

He let me hear that cry, let me find my error. If I was to be faulted, it was for want of respect for my mind. But the other doctors didn't think I had one. Records show that each echoed his predecessor's judgment of my intelligence as average. Was that why none ever challenged my courage? But Dr. Finkelstein did. The day I admitted I enjoyed taking the medications his psychiatrist colleague Dr. Board had prescribed: "Really?" he asked with a kindly, half-pitying smile.

Oh, what skill to allow that slight tinge of contempt—did he even know he felt it?—to mingle with his sympathy. The value of an inadvertent look! No overzealous badgering. (You want peo-

ple to think, Poor thing, she can't help herself?) None of that
would work. Just the timely delivery of a "really," and I was on my
way.

Toward the end of the fall semester, my early memories began
to storm back with greater force than I could control. Dr. Finkelstein saw it coming before I did: "Carol, why don't you go over to
the hospital?" Then, sensing my despair: "You think this is just
another failure, don't you? It's anything but."

I was admitted to Allen Memorial Hospital in Waterloo between the fall and spring semesters of '72. Medical records,
penned by Dr. Board, indicate that Payne Whitney's discharge
diagnosis of my "chronic undifferentiated schizophrenia" had
changed to the "schizo-affective subtype," characterized by acute
melancholic episodes alternating with severe emotional distur-
bance. Dr. Board, who recorded my symptoms as "depression,
anxiety, disorganization of thinking, and dissociative episodes of
crying," treated them with Tofranil, Thorazine, Stelazine, and in-
termuscular injections of the relaxant Vistaril.

Those are the facts. Here is the experience:

During a group therapy session a fellow patient, hearing the
story of my childhood, wagged her head with the comment,
"Look at that. She spent her whole life in a dark closet."

And suddenly I broke the lock. Screams stifled for thirty-
seven years rushed out of me like buried fire. I was engulfed by
wave after wave of terror. My screams gave no warning; before I
had time to run out of the room, another was under way. Always,
I was asked to return and thanked for my consideration by the
staff member present.

I could not enter the bathroom unattended without screaming.

"What must have happened there?" I asked Dr. Finkelstein, in a calmer moment. He shrugged. The actual memory might surface, and it might not. What did it matter, as long as my feelings were breaking free? His thinking was not only correct but keen.

Once, during visiting hours, I saw a plump, smiling bald man I was certain was my father. My terror must have frightened the visitors. Again I was asked to leave the room. Mindful of being in the hands of a caring, dedicated staff, I understood why. They always told me when Dr. Board or Dr. Finkelstein called to ask how I was. When I pleaded with the day nurse going off duty, "Where are you going? Take me with you," she knew I'd become a little girl again, pleading with my mother to take me with her to the store.

One night I began stretching out into what I feared was a catatonic stupor, but which turned out to be a muscle spasm from too much medication. I broke the rigidity midway by a scream. Given a shot of Visteril, followed by repeated injections of the sleeping medication Somnos, I traipsed into the kitchen at 4 A.M. for yet my third snack when Nurse Claudia marveled: "How you can still navigate!" We laughed at the middle-aged three-year-old searching the house for her mother. But Claudia was no Barbara; Claudia was kind.

I asked Dr. Finkelstein if he thought I could make friends with her after I left the hospital.

"Let her be your nurse," he answered. A wonderful nurse who had only to look at me to sense an oncoming wave of terror. Then she'd lead me quickly to a punching bag that I'd beat in rhythm to the shouted prayer, "Health, strength, and confidence!" again and again and again. I blessed the utterance of despair, the act that achieves mercy.

Loree visited all the time, bringing, with my toiletries and clothing, textbooks for the spring semester. I may have been flailing around in mid-ocean but with students registering for classes, it was time to drag myself to shore. What a friend! Is it odd that despite her, Claudia, and Dr. Finkelstein, my loneliness never felt keener? The more I had, the more I craved; the more I craved, the more I wrote. With loneliness nourished on relationships, my healthy grief bore fruit, not once but many times.

I'd have stayed longer at Allen Memorial if I could. I think now of Grete from Gracie Square, Iris from Payne Whitney—young, flesh in full blossom—screaming down the halls of some state institution. If they'd come in time to a place like this! And Alice, silent Alice, whose suffering earns no distinction because it has no tongue. What words does she make for herself? Does she still make words?

Several colleagues came to visit, and of course news of my hospitalization spread. My teaching left much to be desired. No contract renewal had been promised, and none came. Instead, I was offered a tenure-track post at Utica College in upstate New York.

Saying good-bye to Dr. Finkelstein was the hardest thing I remember. I didn't think I'd ever see him again. With no other doctor, no other man, had I ever felt at home.

~

Arriving in Utica several weeks before the fall semester, I settled into an apartment, but searched in vain for a therapist. The main medical facility rejected me point-blank. How was it put? "We lack the resources to accommodate you." Nor would they suggest an outside doctor. With my month's supply of medicine dwindling and classes soon to begin, I made a quick call to Dr. Finkelstein, who directed me to a Syracuse psychiatrist, Dr. Sherwin S. Radin.

Every Monday, Wednesday, and Saturday for the next three years, strangers saw a fattish, middle-aged woman standing on a dark Genesee Street corner at 6:30 A.M. hailing down the Syracuse bus. That two-hour ride back and forth in the snowbelt of the nation—how it dragged on my nerves! I'd sit up front with the driver, who joked about U-turning us down to the tropics: "Just you and me, kid." After the local Sunday paper ran an essay about me, I hopped on his Monday morning bus. "That's me!" I said, pointing to my photo.

"Like a little girl," remarked Dr. Radin later.

It was so difficult getting started with yet another rundown of my life, another yellow legal pad resting on another oversized desk. Sedate, stately Dr. Radin, eager to preserve my balance, resolved to keep me out of the hospital. We'd focus on my difficulties teaching, in finding publishers, in losing weight. In Utica I was the heaviest I'd ever been. Hunger gnawed away with the realization that at thirty-eight, a woman with my medical history had little hope of forming a lasting tie. The thought invaded me like a persistent friend reminding me that time was closing in. But loneliness had been my friend since before I could remember. It prodded me to excel in my studies when my other hopes were laid to rest. Why now should they stir up again?

I'd have to make do with kindly Dr. Radin, who urged me to find strength in my work. He was most interested in my poems. And like a child bringing gifts to her father, I brought him everything I wrote. "Did you make a copy for me?" he'd ask. No other doctor had shown such interest in my work. Perhaps we both knew I was returning from very rough waters to the only haven I had. And, really, it wasn't so bad. As miserable as I was, I was fortunate: I had a job, a career, good associations with colleagues.

It pleased me, whenever my poems and stories were published, that Dean Carol Guardo dropped notes of congratulations in my mailbox. A single woman, formerly a psychologist, Carol was fascinating to talk to. But our infrequent dinners were not enough. Not enough! Nothing was ever enough. Yet wasn't this what I'd wanted: to cherish my unfulfilled longings, mine them for my poems?

⌒

Dr. Radin listened with special attention the day I mentioned casually, because I didn't think it important, that I'd never had the impulse to stretch out rigid until I saw someone in the hospital do so. "Elena—she seemed lovely to me." That night I saw myself in a dream—young, large, and beautiful, like her. In my hand was a glass of chlorpromazine. Someone above was watching. I didn't make a move. My voices still were silent, my visions came only in dreams. One night the Virgin Mary took me to sleep in her arms.

Toward the end of my second year in Utica, I phoned Dr. Radin more and more. He was always there, always kind. I was still spending half the night writing out my lectures in longhand. And what with traveling to Syracuse in the mornings and teaching in the afternoons, my writing had begun to suffer. Dr. Radin suggested I have my students read their papers aloud. "Let *them* do the presenting." But I couldn't trust myself to listen on my feet. Anyway, I was teaching them to write. I had to nitpick words on the page.

"You don't have to take it *that* seriously," he said.

Oh, no? Teach with my left hand and expect to compose with my right? What should I do with my conscience? Like Dr. Zohrman, did he think it a problem? The truth is, I'd have preferred not to teach at all. But to pay his bills, I had to. Then I must simply learn to endure. But while my creativity blossomed during periods of acute suffering, depression killed it.

In the summer of '74, on the heels of my fortieth birthday, I

saw the figure of Jesus in the center of a twirling fan. I phoned
Dr. Radin in terror. The next day he assured me we'd get through
this together in his office. He increased my dosages of Thorazine
and Haldol and suggested that since classes were out, I see him
four times a week. "Try to remember where it began," he urged.
What's *it?* I asked. "Hallucinations," he replied. Did I ever have
them before? A few scattered memories surfaced; then I remembered no more. I was too frightened. But Carol Guardo, to whom
I'd confessed my fears, tried to dispel them. "Let Him come," she
urged. "Your visions might portend something positive."

That my dean, a trained psychologist, should urge me to trust
what my psychiatrist warned me to fear! Diametrically opposed
viewpoints from these two respected professionals sent me ea-
gerly to the library. I was combing the religious and psychiatric
shelves for information on the subject the very day I was told my
teaching contract would not be renewed. I was hardly surprised,
though my colleagues were astonished when the college awarded
me yet a third summer writing grant for fiction. Encouraged to
stay on a fourth year, I happily refused. Two offers had come
quickly my way: one, a tenure-track position in creative writing at
Ohio's Bowling Green University; the other, a one-semester appointment at New York University, which I accepted.

New York was my home, and I missed it. Since my family had
moved to Florida in the early seventies, I'd visited them bian-
nually. I flew down again that summer to find Jani and Bob,
still childless, taking excellent care of my mother, somewhat to
the exclusion of my stepfather, Charles. He was eighty-two, she,
seventy-four. "Your mother's welfare means everything to me, as
it should to you," declared Charles to me one evening over cock-
tails. Then to my amazement he proposed I give up teaching and
move in with her before he left. "Where are you going?" I asked.

"Back to New Jersey," he said. "I want to die near my sons."

"And I'm to be sacrificed for that?" I asked him bluntly.

"It's your place as a single woman," he insisted.

I wasn't unsympathetic to his needs. But mindful of Dr. Finkelstein's warning to keep my family at a distance, I simply said no, and left the next day for New York City.

No sooner had I found an apartment than I telephoned my old acting friends with the news that I'd be teaching Creative Writing to Theatre Artists. To which one replied, "Why not Creative Writing for Shoemakers? The principles are the same, aren't they?" Indeed they are, I laughed. But I had come secretly for another reason. The first Saturday in my new apartment, I dialed Dr. Sapirstein's number. For years I'd longed to tell him how well his "idiot child" had done. Now was my chance.

"This is amazing!" he exclaimed. "I never come in on Saturdays! I was just taking a walk in the neighborhood, and decided to check my mail."

"I'm teaching at NYU now," I boasted happily. "Will you see me?"

"Absolutely. You were a beautiful girl," he added.

It was 1975. Nineteen years had passed since our first interview. I was forty-one, he sixty-one. His old office was just as I remembered it—and he was, too, though somewhat balder and slightly portlier. "You haven't changed a bit," I told him, swinging into my old seat with confidence.

In response to my accomplishments, I received a few poker-faced "very goods"; to my frequent hospitalizations, a more animated "I knew it! Your symptoms were classic."

"In what way?"

He waved a hand—don't ask. Then, "You know, as an attractive woman, marriage still lies within your power."

Was that so? I picked up my cue: "Tell me, do you still think a woman should wait six to twelve dates before sleeping with a man?"

"Times have changed," he yawned.

"You were so angry with me for sleeping with Henry," I reminded.

"It's all right. I forgive you."

"You forgive me?"

"Gimme one o' your cigarettes." As I rose to do so, he fumbled for something in his side drawer. Pulling out a sheet of paper, he exclaimed, "Here! My granddaughter wrote this, a condolence note to a friend of ours. Isn't it wonderful? She's only eight years old."

I could have done as well. I asked for my bill then and there. Truly, I must have been crazy to have yearned for the approval of this man whose paternal blessing I still craved. But so in thrall was I to my needs, to say nothing of his professional credentials, that though I'd been progressing steadily forward, I fell back and was jolted up again by a reality I'd not otherwise have faced: From then on I would watch my step.

With prescriptions from Dr. Radin, I'd muddle through the next few months without a doctor. But I needed Dr. Finkelstein and had somehow to get back to him. I'd applied for a visiting appointment in fiction writing that spring at the University of Wisconsin at Madison. A month later the offer came through. Yes, Dr. Finkelstein would take me on again. I would catch a bus from Madison to Waterloo, something to look forward to every other Saturday.

But, oh, those Friday nights on the road, hour after hour, bumping through tiny Midwestern towns, two-minute spins through Main Streets with their flickering neon signs: Chinese Restaurant

. . . Jesus Saves . . . Old Ladies Home . . . Welcome to Milwaukee
Brew . . . Repent! God Still Loves You Anyway . . . Orphanage for
Boys. I'd stay over at Waterloo's Quality Inn, where, weather permitting, Loree would drive in from Cedar Falls to meet me for
dinner. Otherwise we'd talk on the phone. I couldn't burden her
any more with my problems. Dick had taken his life barely a year
ago—beloved husband, father, and professor. His writing had
dried up, so one night he shut the garage door and turned on the
ignition. And his breast-beating colleagues were still moaning,
"What a failure on our part to love."

"Baloney!" I told Dr. Finkelstein. "I was furious with him. He
left Loree with three of his children! Why didn't he smash into a
tree? With no insurance money, she's caring for five children
now, teaching full time, buying day-old bread. My God! You want
to check out? Have some consideration for the people you leave
behind."

Was that Carol talking? Yes. We do grow sometimes.

My visions of Jesus remained: a hand, a foot, the slim, luminous image of His nose, the shadow of His crown. Then His complete figure appeared upside down on the cross. Dr. Finkelstein
alerted my attending psychiatrist, Dr. Board, who increased my
Haldol. When I asked Dr. Board if he thought I was having hallucinations, he looked askance at me:

"What are you asking? Whether Jesus is really visiting you?"

Too ashamed to say yes, I mumbled, "Maybe."

To which he rejoined, "Upside down?"

I'd had no religious training. Nor had I ever read the New Testament. Had I known that Saul of Tarsus—later the Apostle
Paul—was blinded by visions of Jesus on his way to Damascus,
or that Jesus' disciple Simon Peter, the "rock" of the church, had
at his own request been crucified upside down, I'd have taken it

as a call to convert. Instead, half blind and in pain, I took my medicine.

Having been asked to teach the following year at Madison, I spent a productive summer at MacDowell. But back at school that fall, my visions continued to blind me. I was too troubled to write more than a few minutes at a time. Sometimes I could barely see my way to class. I told my students I had a noncontagious eye infection that made it difficult to read, and trained myself to listen to them read their work aloud.

On one of my frequent visits to the emergency room of University Hospital, a doctor, finding nothing wrong with my eyes, asked what medications I was on. I told him I was seeing a therapist in Iowa. "Why Iowa?" he asked brusquely.

"Because there's someone there I trust."

He left the room to get some drops, when I overheard him explain to someone that my "blinding hallucinations" could be traced to some original trauma or other. Where he got his information, I don't know. I never gave permission for my hospital records to be passed about.

The summer of '77 I was invited back to MacDowell, where my visions gave no trouble and my writing progressed. Then two more job offers came through: a temporary post at Scripps College in Claremont, California, and a tenure-track position at University of Kansas, which I accepted.

Chapter Nineteen

*K*ansas in August on a long, hot trek from the grocer, just before classes began. No breath of air was stirring. Huge grasshoppers were shooting for my heels. I paid scant attention to the passing cars, the curious stares of drivers, as I lugged home packages of food in my two-wheeled, New York shopping cart before a forecasted storm.

Another was rankling within. Three weeks earlier I'd arrived from the MacDowell Colony only to learn that Menninger's had scheduled my battery of psychological tests with Dr. Skollar to conflict with my first KU English Department meeting. When I phoned my assigned psychiatrist, Dr. Sampson, to protest. "Carol, life is tough," he replied. Is that why I'd done so poorly?

The sun was beating down. Parched and itching from Thorazine, I couldn't walk any faster. I didn't want to go home; the air-conditioning was down. And the previous week a heavy rain had caused water to leak through the substandard floors of my ground-floor "luxury" apartment. Mud everywhere underfoot, my books and papers in disarray, furniture ruined, I couldn't work or sleep. Fearing rats and mice, I'd asked the management to lend me an upstairs space, but they refused.

"You're very angry," remarked Dr. Sampson at our first interview. "Why don't you let 'em have it? *They* can't do you any harm."

Step on the right toes, avoid the wrong ones? I grumbled, turning the corner to my house. To weigh all our acts for their therapeutic value is enough to keep everyone sick! No, I didn't exactly think these words, but felt them all the more for my inability to express them. The clouds were beginning to gather.

~

Two months later. The mud had dried, my belongings were again in place. And the psychologist Sheila Skollar's conviction that I'd be unable to give a coherent lecture flew in the face of the fact that, for the first time, my classes were going beautifully. Who knew why? And after nine years of lessons, I'd finally learned to drive! Dr. Sampson was pleased. What was there to discuss? I'd entertain him with funny stories. He was keenly interested in "the masochism of Jewish humor." Oh, he was a folksy soul, no stand-offishness about him. Once I kept him laughing for fifty minutes, thanked him, and walked out.

Sometimes on lonely nights, I'd cry out to him on the phone —"wild cries" he made sure later to remind me—that I wanted something to hold. Get a dog, he told me. And I did: a sweet little six-month-old mutt I named Gobo.

I remember a brief affair with Dr. Sampson's colleague, forensic psychiatrist, Dr. Frankel, to whom a colleague of mine had introduced me.

"You know, on all that medication, even the orgasms are boring," I complained one day in session.

"Really?"

"Your friend depresses me. I don't know why."

"Because he himself is depressed—chronically depressed. Don't repeat that. If you do, I'll deny having said it."

Brawny, cheerful Dr. Sampson, you didn't have to remind me you could lie with impunity.

Two weeks before Christmas break, I invited Dr. Frankel to dinner for the last time. After coffee, he lurched back in his chair right on Gobo's paw. He didn't excuse himself; but while I was examining it for damage, he asked if I knew how tiny my puppy's brain was or how utterly and completely he worshipped me: "You're God to him, you know that?" and when I made no reply, in a cooing voice sighed, "He keeps you company, doesn't he?"

In some shadowed recess of my brain an old scar began to itch and burn.

With weekends free to write, I didn't know why I kept watching the clock until it was time to eat, walk the dog, or sleep. At times my will was eager, but the fire that kindled it gave out. It needed something to fan the flames.

That spring I attended a debate in our university auditorium between the psychiatrists Thomas Szasz and Walter Menninger. There I heard Dr. Menninger refer to the mentally ill as "the offending ones."

"Did he really say that?" I asked my neighbor.

"Yes."

He seemed to be dozing onstage. Next day I wrote him a letter on University of Kansas stationery protesting his cavalier dismissal of people like me. He never responded.

At year's end, my department chairman asked whether I cared to be considered the following fall for early promotion and tenure. I was honored. I'd already been invited to MacDowell for June '78, when I received an invitation from a professor in the Psychology Department to a party, which Sheila Skollar had also been asked to attend. Accepting, I fantasized instantly the entire Psychology Department buzzing with the news that their paranoid colleague over in English was thriving. *This* party would be worth attending. But no sooner had I entered the door than my hostess told me that Sheila couldn't come: "Last minute babysitting problems," she explained. Before or after she learned I'd be there? I knew better than to ask.

No, I argued to Dr. Sampson, this was more than a disappointment to my ego. Last summer she'd wanted me in the hospital. Would Dr. Skollar not learn from her mistake? Perhaps on seeing me she wouldn't have thought it one—but not even to venture to find out?

"Look, everyone makes mistakes," he said. "And remember, *I* didn't go along with her recommendation, did I?" He settled comfortably back in his chair. That's right, I thought; appease me by praising yourself. *Ego uber Alles.* I was too angry to speak. He tried to convince me my feelings were unreasonable, and reaching for his prescription pad, informed me he was increasing my Thorazine. How dare he? Was my anger some aberration unrelated to a cause?

"You can't help it," he said. Oh, what benevolent contempt! "What's wrong?" he persisted. "What's *wrong* with taking pills? I'm here, I'll be here."

On what assumption is such comfort given, but that I'm ill and will always remain so? That was wrong, nothing more.

At the end of the academic year, after agreeing to join my parents on their cruise, I left a message at the Menninger switchboard that I was terminating therapy. Dr. Sampson called twice. A friendly letter followed. Then Dr. Frankel phoned. How was I feeling? Fine, busy. I hung up. It rang again.

"Dr. Sampson here." I steeled myself. "What happened?"

"When?" I joked.

"You're ill!"

"I don't agree." Did I imagine he was out to get me? No, only to keep me—a patient first, and a person second. And what a perfect one I was! Never late, neither I nor my payments.

"I don't need you *or* your medicine."

"This isn't the first time you've fired me," he bristled.

"Don't wait around."

Then, "It is my professional opinion that you are sounding grandiose."

"Really? You think I think I'm omniscient? Look to yourself, Dr. Sampson. It's not omniscience we need, it's omnicompetence."

The next day I got an unlisted phone number. Three weeks later, after a brief stint at MacDowell, I joined my parents aboard the cruise ship *Sagafjord*, where, on the first night at sea, I tossed my pills to the waves.

~

How did it feel at first? Starving people who speak of a hunger beyond words would know. I remember transports from fierce anguish to quick, sharp ecstasies. I had visions of Christ bathed in light and heard the words, "However much you protest, I am your brother, your servant, and your friend."

Then came another unearthly voice: "I am James; I come bearing light."

Of my prayers, spoken or written, one remains in my mind: that my labor contain the seeds of its fruit for the nourishment of souls. I woke next morning in the midst of a heavenly light and saw the enormous eye of God weeping in agony. This was followed by a vision of my earthly father holding my head to his chest, as he did when I was a child, saying: "Little *chayalah*, little *chayalah*," which in Hebrew means "little animal."

Visions were given to me that let me know where I'd been since the day of his death. All things cloudy seemed suddenly luminous and precise. I dreamed of entering symphonies, entering shrines; I'd start an artistic revolution in the name of science, its weapons, words, and music. I would learn the grammar of music, master the mathematics of the dance.

On deck one morning before sunrise, I saw a giant rising waist high in midocean. Vision or hallucination? It was possible I was having both. I turned quickly away and afterward kept close to my cabin.

And all the while, Mother kept complaining, "You're not mingling!"

"Don't you want to make your way?" chipped in Charles.

On the evening of my forty-fourth birthday, I went to the lounge for a drink and had a marvelous talk with a crew member, who later joined me in my cabin. I was so alive, so horribly needy, I tremble at the memory. It was the last affair I would have.

~

Back at school that fall, I knew I must be scrupulously careful with feelings and reactions when others were around. The need to speak, to communicate, became so exquisitely painful I felt it stop up by the force of the impulse itself. And the realization washed over me like an inner tidal wave that I'd been crippled by an excess of need. Without the safety valve of medication, my rage swelled hand in hand with joy—the fierce joy of knowing I'd been right from the start: I *had* needed a place to scream *before* I could reason out that need with a doctor.

At this time, a commercial editor (now dead) who had long admired my fictional accounts of mental illness asked me to write a personal memoir on the subject; he'd consider offering me a contract on the basis of a satisfactory outline and sample chapter. This I took as divine intervention: I was ready to succeed. By day I taught my classes, and at night let the floodgates open. The work felt dictated. It seemed so right, I didn't even bother to proofread. By Thanksgiving it was done.

The partial manuscript in the mail, my tenure application submitted, my hopes burst into fantasies of world fame: onrushes of thoughts and feelings, insane wanderings of mind, despite which, my classes continued to thrive. In a heightened state of consciousness I could pinpoint, as never before, problems in my students' manuscripts.

At night I telephoned people from my past. Martha from Payne Whitney remarked that I was speaking very quickly. "Because I'm thinking quickly."

"Are you thinking *too* quickly?" she asked.

"Too quickly for *whom?*" I burst back. "We were brainwashed, don't you understand?"

Next, I tried an actress I hadn't spoken to for twenty years: "I'd have called sooner," I began, "but I forgot your last husband's name . . . I mean your husband's last name!"

She roared, of course, but then a few minutes later: "Carol, are you all right?"

That same question came from others. I had to speak to someone who knew me. Who but Dr. Finkelstein? Why hadn't I called him right away?

After I'd told him what I'd done "Please," I asked. "Could you tell me simply and clearly what was wrong?"

A brief pause. "You're too intense."

"I don't understand."

"You threaten people, Carol, and they want to attack you—or run away: whichever."

"But students are breaking their necks to get into my classes."

"They know those will end soon."

"But they enjoy being there at the time!"

"They know it's only for a little while."

"Dr. Finkelstein, I don't know what you're saying to me. Talk to me—please talk to me. Because we never really talked, you know, not about this. You just sat there and allowed me to love you, and told me there was no need to feel anxious about it. Now I'm asking you why it was necessary to pay you for that privilege."

"Carol, you're too intense."

"Please! Explain yourself! Things have to be clear, absolutely clear right now. Right now!"

"You're not letting me talk."

"I'm sorry . . . Well?"

"Well in certain schizophrenic disorders—"

"No! Speak English, not psychoanalese! You know you people really ought to read more. Don't you know when needs get this big you have to get lost in the melody sometimes? What I mean— I mean Shakespeare knew more than Freud; he even said it better!"

"You're still thinking logically," he said quietly.

"Well, so are you. You're just not making yourself clear. Say something else."

"You want it straight?"

"Absolutely straight."

"Your needs are frightening."

"What am I supposed to *do* with that piece of information, Dr. Finkelstein, just sit here?"

"Carol, you asked me for it." A jeweled silence. "Are you all right?"

"Did you *have* to ask me that? Speak again!"

"Okay—here we go. I went to a performance the other night of *Long Day's Journey*. Carol, it was so powerful, so lyrical, so absolutely heartrending that . . . well, I walked out exhausted."

"You walked out exhausted?"

"Yes."

"Dr. Finkelstein, don't break my heart."

Not long after, I received word that the New York editor couldn't

offer me a contract on the basis of the memoir chapter I'd submitted. He'd have to see a longer excerpt. This, on top of the news
that I'd been voted down that year for early promotion and
tenure (I received them the next) ignited a rage so vast, I refused
to speak to my colleagues. I felt, wrongly, I was being toyed with.
That Ph.D.'s with published books and far more teaching experience than I had been voted down for years meant nothing. But
when my chairman reminded me that he hadn't forced me to accept his invitation to apply, I realized I was overreacting and apol-
ogized. I'd apply again next year on condition that, during it, I'd
be excused from teaching to write and give readings around the
country. And to this he consented.

In the meantime, with my feelings out of control, I knew
enough to drop the memoir. Still, my motor had been gunned.
In the privacy of my home, I relived my entire life alone. At times
my suffering was so acute, I didn't think I could bear it; at others, rage took over, a delicious rage, not too overwhelming for me
to realize I was employing it for the sake of knowing exactly what
had gone wrong. Only that the need to explain remain greater
than the pain of explaining!

First, I asked what part I had played in my illness. To what had
my seeing eye gone blind? Fear of insanity means what? Not the
temporary loss of control I'd experienced at Allen Memorial Hospital, but the terror of not finding it again. The endless torment
I'd feared for Grete I no longer feared for myself. Where was I at
fault? Yes, I was victimized in childhood; yes, my silence was a
long-term effect of it. But I myself was no victim—or never felt
myself one. The word connoted spinelessness, a worse mark of
shame in my family, *and* in the postwar fifties, than schizophrenia itself (which, paradoxically, came into fashion ten years later
with the critic Leslie Fiedler's legendary complaint that the youth

of the sixties worshipped the schizophrenic rather than the sage). Was it my vanity alone that insisted victims don't want responsibility and I did? The fact that I was raised to punish myself for everything didn't mean I wasn't wrong in *some* things.

Why didn't I shout out sooner my objections to a diagnostic label that reduced me to a set of symptoms my professional success belied? My thinking was prejudged disorganized; were my thoughts also senseless? Like Alice, I kept them to myself. From contempt? Perhaps in part; call us crazy long enough, we oblige and act accordingly. But by my silence, whom was I appeasing? Those in my early childhood who had wanted me out of the way? Caught in the toils of memory, my rage rekindled. I took a deep breath and went on: How often had I gone crazy appeasing the sensibilities of the sane? But if I chose insanity by default, in its throes, where was the choice I couldn't see?

Ah, there was the lie! For I *had* glimpsed "intellectually" that my real aim, to stay sick, was at odds with my declared aim, to thrive. But I lacked the courage to confront it. Now, with the heartfelt realization that my need to be cared for conflicted with my need to succeed, I asked again, where was my help? Weren't my failed efforts to grow abetted by well-meaning doctors who, cultivating my dependence, reinforced the lie that I couldn't thrive without them *or* their pills, which muffled the needs they urged me to express. And by so activating my feelings, only to shut them off, didn't they render me unable to connect my distress to the circumstances that caused it? This they called "dissociation," that "classic symptom" of schizophrenia, and grew fat on the profits.

It still rankles to remember good Dr. Zohrman's words: "If you expected less of yourself, people would like you better." Did he think me too ill to strive? On first prescribing my pills, he had judged my mind disorganized because it clashed with the confusions in his own. In assuming from my early abuses my impulse to abuse others, he had upset my thinking entirely.

He believed I was out to destroy the world! And even supposing I was, and because of it avoided other people, why did he fault my conscience? Did he never consider that the violence done to me in childhood had instilled not the will to commit it, but a hatred of it in all forms? "Those to whom evil is done / Do evil in return"* sometimes only to themselves.

He hospitalized me to keep me alive. But there I grew much worse. How quickly the tide of grief can turn into a wellspring of hate. I am not the first ex-patient to report that conditions in most mental hospitals are breeding grounds for the eruption of psychotic behavior, but I hope to be among the last. How many of us misdiagnosed in the late fifties remain stigmatized with the schizophrenic label? If these hospitals could serve instead, as Allen Memorial did for me, as temporary stopping-off places—havens for the release of intolerable feelings before they have time to twist inward—what would become of our stigma?

$\sim$

At school the truth was out about my medical history. My colleagues' discomfort in my presence fed my fear that at any moment I might snap out of control. I had only to pass through the halls for conversations to stop. Suddenly everyone began discussing the weather! One day at the mailboxes I spoke up: "Fellas," I said, "look at the calendar; it's February: dress up warm. If you get *too* warm, take your scarves off." Their sharp laughter relieved the tension. But most were frightened; I saw it in the careful way they handled me.

---

*From W. H. Auden's poem "September 1, 1939."

This awkwardness might have passed with time. I was uncomfortable for another reason. I lacked the generosity of spirit to love, or even to like, teaching. So to appease my overzealous conscience, I took overzealous care with student manuscripts, leaving little energy for mine.

In 1984, four years after my promotion and tenure, I was commissioned to write a play about the Watergate heroine Martha Mitchell. Was it possible I was nearly fifty? There was so much I still had to write. After thirteen years of full-time teaching, I gave up my tenure to do so.

Epilogue

*A*nd what since? I moved back to New York, living first at the Y, then for the next eight years in a modest Brooklyn studio where a visiting former colleague remarked that I'd taken a vow of poverty. It was hardly extreme. With a small annuity earned from my years of teaching, and income from readings and workshops, I paid the rent and had enough to eat.

My chastity was no great sacrifice, either. After fifty, the blood doesn't fret so much anymore. Someone reminded me recently that years ago it was difficult for men to be interested in my mind; I had other, more noticeable attributes. That was no longer so. As a result, and to my great joy, friendships with men became possible.

In 1987, my orphan manuscripts still traveling the chilly mails, an offer came through for the publication of my first book, and the following year, for two of my plays. The events since—if I may call them that—have been internal.

Occasionally, on a lonely Sunday, I'd attend services in a nearby Catholic Church in my predominantly Jewish neighborhood. Why? It was a place to go, somewhere I felt comfortable. One morning during Mass I closed my eyes in the midst of a prayer and saw a serpent, sick and pale, turn on its back and disappear into the earth. What did this mean? A few nights later I heard again, "I am James; I come bearing light."

I must say I found it odd, if this *was* a hallucination, that it was of someone who, in my eagerness for the Gospel stories, I had glanced past. My New Testament index listed three Jameses. Which had "spoken"? Matthew's brother, James the Little; John's brother, Jesus' cousin James the Greater; or James the brother of the Lord, first Bishop of Jerusalem, and hence the first Jewish Christian, to whom the "Epistle of James" is attributed? I now read his passionate commitment to social justice and to the doctrine of faith by works and imagined it was he who had "noticed" me. Still, I did nothing.

My past continued to haunt me. I staggered under the weight of memories that fury alone could lift—belated, unreasonable fury at literally everyone who had shamed into permanent suppression my ability to love.

"I am James; I come bearing light." What did he want me to see?

How many days had I passed without a word to anyone, days I could have used, had sadness not forbidden it, to bind my will to work? How long would I fret my life out over disappointments? That I would answer my own mating call, I'd long known. I was doing the work I wanted. What more did I expect? Wasn't it something of a miracle I was no longer ill? I had only to pick up a newspaper to read of horrors much worse than mine. I'd learned to think, to see feelingly—to come alive! Yes, work *was* all; but that is a great deal. I must cherish and protect it. Unless I learned to forgive, my fury would burn it out. Hadn't it happened before?

Yes, I had courage to deny what was false, but I didn't know what was true. The mind is a delicate instrument easily strained and broken and easier, still, to crush. How near I'd been to succumbing! With the help of God, my genes, and Dr. Finkelstein, I'd gained the insight to realize, and the strength to bear, before it was too late, that I had chosen the instruments of my destruction. I wasn't ill; I was soul-sick from the cruelties around me! I'd known it a lifetime, and it weighed on me like lead. Use it! How? Understand its perpetrators. And then what? Forgive and forget? Not so fast: it is *because* I cannot forget what I take the trouble to forgive, that I'm obliged to understand it.

First I would enter my mother's past—hers, my sister's, my father's. I'd then recall instances of their abuse of me *from their points of view,* not in order to condone but to understand—to feel into, to know—the workings of their minds and hearts. My obligation to my work became my obligation to myself. I'd come boldly and brusquely to the facts of my mother's shame over want and early poverty, the circumstances that drove her to see nothing in human nature but its sores; my father's immense loneliness; my sister's early misery. This in order to see, and if possible make conscious in others, truths I had so long hidden from myself. I'd let nothing torment me from the task.

Shortly after I began it, my stepfather Charles separated from my mother and died, as he wished, in the home of one of his sons. He was ninety-seven. Seven years later, my mother passed on in a Florida retirement home at age ninety-six. Jan and Bob remain in Florida; he, retired from his stockbrokerage activities, she, from family cares.

∼

I suppose it's easier to assume that loneliness called forth my visions and voices, than to believe the most improbable of possibilities true: that Jesus, Mary, and James really came to me. Would that be so very frightening? I ask because the media have us so thoroughly convinced that diagnosed "paranoid schizophrenics"—all loners like me—hear voices telling them to do dreadful things, whereas mine just urged me to keep struggling.

How do I explain them? I don't. Nor will I make a case for or against their existence. Only this: the need that created them might also have invited them. To think me mad for having them is an error born of fear.

Perhaps our American fascination with madness is a defense against our fear of it. Why else are we so eager to label—and so distance ourselves from—states of being we don't understand? Or assume that so-called abnormal states of mind lead necessarily to abnormal behavior? Don't these differ?

I don't know whether, having experienced visions, I am more or less qualified to discuss them than scientists whose theories on hallucinations most laymen take on faith. That mine were diagnosed "benign" (as opposed to malignant?) doesn't do them much honor. How any force that contributed to my recovery could be symptomatic of my disease remains beyond me. As does the bovinely parochial assumption, so insulting to the imagination, that visions stem from infirm minds. Had Teresa of Avila seen Christ in the flesh, she'd probably first have gone mad from fear. He came *through* her imagination and, for very different reasons, through mine, too, perhaps. Fact or fiction? I don't know. This much I know: the sane among us are frightened—too frightened to distinguish the psychopath "ordered by God" from the receiver of visual blessings. Back in sixteenth-century Spain, St. Teresa's confessors deemed her visions the work of Satan. Given that her biographers judged her "highly neurotic," I wonder, were she among us today, at what facility she'd be resting, and on what miracle drugs of choice.

Not until those drugs were out of my system was I able to come fully alive. Alive! I was almost trembling. I laugh now with old friends who still remind me that at the time, I nearly drove them crazy. I can well believe it. In flight to Mt. Olympus, I was suddenly discovering things they had known for years: "How important human relationships are!" I'd blurt out suddenly on the phone.

"Carol, I knew that when I was six."

"When I was your age, I was three." That I came safely down from the heights I owe predominantly to them. Friends less patient and forgiving, seeing me out of my shell, told me in subtle ways to go back in; they liked me better the other way. Why? Carol was talking again. Not only was she talking, she was talking out of turn. She used to do that all the time, but now she's saying things we don't like! Oh, that I'd had the courage sooner.

I am well. Do I still have bouts of agony? Of course. I have learned to use them in my work. Despair as nourishment is an old idea; I try to catch it at its flood. I don't always succeed. When it overwhelms me, what then? In order not to do violence to a system that needs temporarily to shut down, I give into it *for a measured period of time.* Then I tell myself, if you don't get to the desk by a certain hour, don't bother to go tomorrow. But I *do* go, and find great joy. I am there now looking out my window at a flitting congregation of clouds. How clear and precise the lines of the world are early in the morning. I have found new ways of seeing. My work and my friends uphold me. I have learned the discipline of happiness. I am the stern and loving taskmaster I longed for.